"Mom's Funny, But Not Ha-Ha Funny"

A Collection of Columns
by
Sally Sotos

Enjoy! Sally

Beagle Boys Books

Mom's Funny, But Not Ha-Ha Funny copyright 2010 by Sally Sotos. All rights reserved. Printed in the United States of America. No part of this book may be used or reproduced in any manner whatsoever without written permission except in the case of reprints in the context of reviews.

ISBN 9781456398989

Cover Art by Dan Colgan and Olive Street Design

Acknowledgements:

I wish to thank my editor and publisher at the Elmhurst Independent: Dee Longfellow and Pete Cruger, respectively. Pete has been especially generous in not charging me a fee for the privilege of taking up space in his newspaper. My appreciation also extends to the readers of the various newspapers in which Pete and Dee have run my column. Several of those readers have taken the trouble of sharing with me their thoughts about my writings. You know who you are, and so do I.

Also, I thank my infinitely patient employer, the law firm of Knight Hoppe, Kurnik and Knight, for affording me an unreasonably generous amount of flexibility in my work schedule over the years.

Finally, my thanks go out to my family -- George, Mary and Maggie -- who encouraged me to write and who have thoughtfully provided me with enough material to fill a book. This book, in fact.

Hope you enjoy reading "Mom's Funny, But Not Ha-Ha Funny." Please buy additional copies for your friends and loved ones: I need to pay for my new kitchen counters.

Sally Sotos
October 2010

Table of Contents:

Foreword

Section One: Modern Living	1
Section Two: Going to the Dogs	9
Section Three: Travel and Adventure	17
Section Four: Beauty, Health and Fashion	43
Section Five: Hearth and Home	62
Section Six: La Famiglia!	85
Section Seven: Food, Glorious Food	114
About The Author	141

Foreword

I didn't really know Sally Sotos very well when she first talked about writing a column for the Independent. I knew she was a business person in downtown Elmhurst and was active on the City Centre Board of Directors, a group which governs, for lack of a better word, the downtown retail area of Elmhurst. The Elmhurst Independent's publisher Pete Cruger knew her well and urged me to work with her on the column, knowing it would be an enhancement to our paper.

What an understatement! I had no idea how humorous Sally could be. She has the perfect combination of self-deprecation and keen insight to delight readers as they no doubt recognize themselves and their own families in her now-legendary words of wisdom and caricature.

Like most of us, Sally clearly draws a great deal of inspiration from her family and the life going on all around her. Her husband George and her two daughters have been a good source of subject matter as she comments on the day-to-day goings-on of family and community. As years go by and kids grow up, as holidays come and go, as marriages get seasoned with age, she has been a relevant observer of all the inner workings and idiosyncrasies of life.

I recall with delight a letter we received from a woman who was a bit put off by Sally's clever wit as she used one column to poke fun at the Greek holiday traditions often endured by her husband George while growing up. George himself called the woman up and was able to win her over.

That's the beauty of this industry. Sometimes you make people mad or sad or uncomfortable. Quite frankly, if we didn't do that, we wouldn't be doing our jobs as a newspaper.

Sally has made that possible, which is why she is a good fit. The Elmhurst Independent congratulates her on the publication of this book and reminds its readers that there may be times when she gets you thinking, gets you angry or gets you squirming in your seat.

But most of all -- she will get you laughing. She will make you recognize yourself in these every day situations and will make you realize, sometimes in the darkest hour, the best thing to do is to keep your sense of humor. Enjoy!

Dee Longfellow
Editor
The Elmhurst Independent

Section 1: Modern Living

Mama Said There'd Be Days Like This
February 27, 2008

"You doing anything else this afternoon?" the handsome optometrist asked casually, while peering at me (or, more accurately, at my eyes) through one of those giant pieces of equipment designed to remind you that your eyesight, along with every other part of your body, is going straight to hell in a handbasket.

Doing anything else? I was flattered. It's been a long time - and we're talking decades now, eons really - since anyone used an obvious pick-up line like that with me. "Well," I began coyly, trying to bat my eyes, "Not really. Why do you ask?"

"It's time we dilated your pupils. I need to check for macular degeneration and cataracts." He began preparing the drops.

I was crestfallen. He wasn't putting the moves on me; he was checking for Old People's Diseases. Great. Then I panicked. "Wait," I said, clutching his arm. "Am I going to have to wear those weird Old People wraparound black sunglasses this afternoon?"

He smiled indulgently. "No, your own will be fine. Now, tilt your head back . . ."

Half an hour later, I was stumbling out into the blindingly bright sunshine. News flash: your own sunglasses are of absolutely no help when your pupils are dilated. I felt like one of the kids in *Indiana Jones and the Temple of Doom*, liberated from years spent underground, blinking and shielding their eyes.

Another news flash: when your pupils are dilated, you look like a maniac. So wouldn't you know, that was the afternoon I had to call the police to report that some idiot hit-and-run driver had creamed my 1988 Buick as it was innocently parked on our street.

Complicating the picture was the fact that I had recently

contracted a bacterial nasal infection, which threw off a powerful putrid aroma, as if an animal had crawled into my head and died there. I was covering the odor with heavy doses of Scope, while also trying not to breathe near anyone.

As a result, the image I presented to the investigating officers was a wild-eyed middle-aged woman who reeked of mouthwash and would only speak out of the corner of her mouth.

Book 'er, Danno. I'm surprised they didn't read me my rights on the spot. I had Probable Cause written all over me.

After the police left, I sighed heavily -- downwind, of course. The bashed-in, undriveable, 20-year-old Buick sitting forlornly on the street made our place look like something out of Tobacco Road. (The Christmas tree still being up, in late January, didn't help.) My dilated eyes made me look like CatWoman, and not in a Halle Berry way. My bacterial breath would make strong men flinch.

"Please, God," I prayed, "Let today not be the day that Daniel Craig drops in for a visit. Any other day - as I've told You repeatedly - would be fine. But please, not today."

People, there is a God, and He answered my prayer. I did not get a visit from Daniel Craig, nor even from Jeremy Irons, whose name had also appeared in some of my prior entreaties to the Lord.

We did, however, get a call at 3:30 a.m., from a police officer on the midnight shift, to inform us that our Buick was in violation of the overnight parking ban, and that it appeared to him to have been the victim of a hit-and-run driver. He was standing in front of our car, and wanted us down there ASAP.

My husband, roused from a deep sleep, trudged out in his Rex Kwan Do zubas and explained the events to the officer, who apologized profusely ("Nobody told me") and drove off.

We sat bleary-eyed at the kitchen table. I blew a kiss to my husband, who smiled, then winced: "Still fighting that sinus infection, eh?"

It Happens
October 22, 2008

So, did you read about the lady in Holland, Ohio, who was cleaning her house on a recent Sunday when the doorbell rings, and guess what? It's Barack Obama, who had decided to do some door-to-door campaigning in her town. Apparently she hadn't gotten the memo. She said later that Sunday was "the one day I come home to clean ceiling fans and I look like crap, and then this happens." Not the kind of change you want to believe in, eh, sister?

And the encounter went further downhill. Barack asked Ms. Ceiling Fans how she was managing during the economic turmoil . . . and she said she was doing fine! "Bummer," he probably thought to himself. "A little hardship would have been helpful, lady. If I'd wanted to visit someone who was doing fine, I'd have dropped in on Bill Gates. At least he wouldn't have looked like crap."

It wasn't supposed to go down like this! Don't candidates have advance teams to prepare the way? This isn't "Candid Camera," for goodness' sake! Where were the Secret Service guys with the dark glasses and earpieces, constantly surveying the block for lunatics?

But wasn't that all so typical? Day after day, you sit at home in your pearls and heels, like June Cleaver, and nobody drops in. Then, the one day you wrap the bad hair in a dirty bandana, pull on the shorts with stains and holes in embarrassing locations, and start scouring the bathroom tile grout with the kids' toothbrush, and what happens? A candidate for leader of the free world strides up the front steps, narrowly missing the dog poop you'd meant to pick up. He raps briskly on the front door, and you pull it open, expecting it to be your neighbor who had just called to borrow a roll of toilet paper.

So there you are, with the bandana and the shorts and the toothbrush and the Charmin, staring at your possible future president and thinking, "Please let this not be happening. Please wake me up now." Meanwhile, he's thinking, "Why did I go into politics?

I was having a nice life where I never had to deal with weirdos like this. Please wake me up now."

But that's the thing about life: you don't wake up. Nobody yells, "And . . . cut! That's a wrap! Great job!" The curtain doesn't fall at the dramatic moment. The scene just keeps going. You stand there and mumble, "I thought you were Sue." He keeps smiling, assuming he's misunderstood what you said. "Sue is my neighbor. She needs toilet paper," you explain, sounding even more like an idiot, if that's possible. He's thinking, "It was a really nice life. I dealt with smart people. Heck, I was smart. I'm getting dumber just standing near this woman."

Finally, he ends the scene by urging you to vote. The door closes, and you instantly think of all the witty and profound things you could have said. The French have a phrase for this: *l'esprit d'escalier*, the stairway moment, describing how you come up with the perfect remark only after you leave the party and you're on your way down the stairs.

On his way back down your front steps, Barack has a stairway moment too. Unfortunately it involves the stuff he had narrowly missed on the way to your door.

It happens.

Neither Here Noir There
August 26, 2009

There I was, lying face down in a pool of drool (hopefully my own), in back of the Jewel loading dock, a broken Jones Soda bottle embedded in my cheek, clad only in a burlap muu-muu I knew wasn't mine. Where'd it come from? I didn't know. I didn't want to know.

I woke up groggily and looked around. As my eyes slowly began to focus, I got my bearings. The memory of the night before was, blessedly, as blank as my checkbook on April 16. Then I remembered the most important thing.

"Jiminy salsa! It's deadline day!"

I stood up, brushed myself off, yanked the glass shards out of my face, swallowed what was left of my pride, and strode purposefully into the Osco, only to be met by the shocked and disgusted glances of shoppers, before they turned away in horror.

"Take a picture; it'll last longer," I snarled, and made my way back to the pharmacy. "Got any Pixie Stix, Joe?" I asked. "Gently used is fine."

He shook his head, reached under the counter, and slid a few over to me. "That's the last time, Sal," he said sternly. "The feds are really cracking down."

"Thanks, Joe," I replied. I slipped into the deserted health food aisle, where I knew I wouldn't be disturbed, and inhaled the magic dust contents deeply. "Mama's gotta sparkle," I whispered.

Outside, I quickly hijacked the first Razor scooter I found, shoving its terrified rider off. "Sorry, kid," I called back over my shoulder as I pedalled maniacally down Schiller. "I've got a deadline to meet."

Finally, I made it home. Not stopping to greet my attack beagles, Incense and Peppermint, who were baying ferociously, I stumbled over to my trusty Macintosh with the 5-inch screen, sat down, and stared grimly.

Three cups of java, two concussions and a rhesus monkey later,

I held the makings of a first draft in my shaking hand.

"Now for some me-time," I grunted. I pulled my battered fedora off its well-worn nail in the wall, and strolled down to my favorite haunt. The guy behind the bar was slowly wiping down the counter with a wet rag. He glanced up at me, nodded, and continued wiping. I slid onto a stool and checked myself for a pulse. Yes!

"Hey, Jimmy," I called, "What's your special today?" "Cake batter with sprinkles, Sal," he replied. "Make it a double, pal," I smiled. "I'm not drivin'."

Jimmy brought me an overstuffed waffle cone. I reached into my muu-muu pocket for a bit of loose change, but found only some washing instructions and a phone number I wasn't about to call. Jimmy stopped me. "It's on the house," he said. "Deadline day, huh?"

"You got it," I nodded, slurping gratefully. Ah: the stuff that dreams are made of. I felt like walking and licking, so I waved goodbye to Jimmy, and headed out the door. As I ambled slowly down the sidewalk, a soft rain began to fall, watering down my ice cream the way that stingy bartender at the Dew Drop Inn waters down my bourbon and branch. He knows I'm allergic to bourbon: it makes me break out in song.

I thought I heard footsteps behind me, but when I looked in the nearby store window reflection, I saw nothing. Either a vampire's tailing me, or my Bel-tone needs a tune-up. I shook my head.

I love this dirty town.

Quit While You're Behind!
October 7, 2009

We advise our kids that winners never quit and quitters never win and all that, but the reality is that there are plenty of times in life when the best thing to do is quit, let it go, give it up, know when to fold 'em, abandon ship. Or at least change course. For example:

Don't stay in the toilet stall after you've discovered it has an unreliable door latch! How many times have you cursed yourself for not immediately walking out of the stall? Instead, you subject yourself to an uncomfortable sojourn in a seated position, leaning far forward to brace the door lest it be nudged open by some ham-handed passerby.

Don't keep using the grocery cart with the crazy wheel! You've worked hard, yanking and pulling, to separate it from the death grip of its jealous fellow carts, as they stand locked together in line. Only then do you discover that the object of your efforts has a crazy wheel, which spins madly on its own, refusing to roll in harmony with the other three. What do you do? You're still there, in the narthex of the supermarket, still within easy access of the other carts, which are lined up like dime-a-dance girls at an old music hall, mutely calling, "Pick me! Pick me!"

You look down at Crazy Wheel and think, "It'll be OK," and start pushing. It's not OK. You expend inordinate effort just to get into the produce section. There's still time to change course: you're not fully committed to this one yet. But do you go back and start over?

No! that would be quitting!

Don't wear the top with the plunging neckline! As you stand in front of the mirror in your bedroom, getting dressed for the big dinner, you cast a critical eye at your reflection. That's a bit more décolletage than you remember when you bought that dress. The older you get, the less acreage people are interested in seeing, really. You bend forward and look in the mirror: this is what the person across the table will be viewing all through a multi-course dinner. Good God! You straighten up quickly. That won't do at all.

      But you really like this dress. Your only alternative is that dowdy thing your mother gave you. You bend ever so slightly forward again, and look up cautiously. Well, that's not as bad. It'll be OK. You'll just have to remember to sit very, very upright during dinner. And off you go.

      The half hour at the open bar passes rather quickly, but you get your money's worth. You relax and begin to enjoy yourself. Soon, you are seated at dinner. My, this soup is good. So aromatic! You inhale appreciatively, then bring your head up and . . .Bring your head up!?! You practically had your nose in the soup! Your spine whips upright to full vertical, and you shoot a panicked glance across the table, where the gentleman's face has a stricken look, as if he has seen the ravages of time laid out before him. Which he has.

      You spend the rest of dinner pretending to scratch a persistent itch on your left shoulder with your right hand.

      Don't pass up that rest stop! The roadside sign bore an ominous warning: "Next Rest Stop 92 Miles." That gives you pause on your road trip, doesn't it? You're not as young as you used to be, and neither is your bladder. Nor is it as reliable as in days of yore. You can't "Depend" on it as much, if you get my drift. You start calculating how long it takes to travel 92 miles. Hmmm. Then you think, "I haven't had that much coffee. It'll be OK." You get closer to the exit. There's still time! There's still time! You drive by defiantly. Next sign: "Road Construction Ahead. Expect Long Delays."

      Uh-oh.

Section 2: Going To The Dogs

Pockets The Wonder Dog
March 5, 2008

When our kids were seven and nine years old, we decided we needed to make the house livelier. That's not quite as stupid as it sounds. My dad had just passed away, the first time death had touched our kids, and we felt the need to fill the house with life, to compensate for the loss of Grandad.

First, we bought fish. At one time, we had fourteen fish tanks in our home. But, people, acquiring fish is not the way to show your kids the wonders of life. It's a really good way to make them nonchalant about death and hesitant to become emotionally attached to others, but that wasn't exactly what we were trying to convey.

Then, we bought birds. They were a little better than the fish, in that they didn't die as often (well, you only die once, but you get my meaning), and they made more noise than the fish, but they still weren't what I'd call cuddly. By the way, that old saw that you don't bite the hand that feeds you, and you don't poop where you eat -- our birds hadn't heard either of those. They did bite, and did poop. Still do.

Then, we got a dog. More accurately, my husband located a beagle puppy, brought the kids with him to pick it up, and then, and only then, presented the idea of getting a puppy, and the puppy itself, to me.

Was that fair? I felt like the Sally Field character in *Mrs. Doubtfire*: the stern parent, the no-fun parent, the rules enforcer. And with good reason: unlike my husband, I'd grown up with dogs, and knew that the parent who's at home more (that would be me), is the one who's in charge of the dog, good intentions and children's promises notwithstanding.

I stipulated that the puppy was here strictly on probation.

Fourteen-plus years later, he's still on probation. We named him Pockets, for reasons still unclear. He had the good sense to become housebroken immediately, thus removing the chief objection to his presence.

He has complied with none of my other rules over the next fourteen years. Before he got too old for it, he jumped up on all the furniture, regarding the couch, comfy chairs, etc., as his personal property, and in fact often indicating his desire, for example, that you vacate the chair you were sitting in so that he could occupy it.

Pockets slept on our bed with us for years, which you should never permit, for the same reasons you should never permit your kids to do so, namely, they take up too much precious space, move around too much, and snore too loud.

Beagles are supposed to be marsh hunting dogs, the kind they use for the L.L. Bean catalog covers, with a pheasant in his mouth. Our beagle only hunts dead animals, and even then has a challenge matching wits with them.

Once we returned home to find half a pound of ham vanished from the kitchen counter, a gnawed wrapper on the floor, and Pockets the only one who'd been in the house the entire time. He maintained eye contact with us as we paced the kitchen floor, as if daring us to hire a forensic canine dentist to check out the bite marks on the wrapper. We speculated aloud that perhaps someone had broken into the house and stolen the ham; Pockets nodded vigorously.

A few years later, a loaf of bread similarly went AWOL. Our theory is that, over time, he's been making himself a series of ham sandwiches; we're waiting for the cheese and the mustard to disappear.

Gradually, the aging process has taken its toll on Pockets, as it has on many of us, although he's a bit farther along the aging curve. He had to have ACL surgery (uninsured); he received chiropractic spinal adjustments; he eventually lost control of his bowels and bladder; and last month he died.

He lived his life surrounded by people who loved him, who were mad crazy about him. We should all be so lucky.

Pockets Sotos was proud that a beagle finally won Best in Show. He himself was best in snow.

Ginger, The Junkyard Dog
August 20, 2008

Did you read recently that actor Kevin Costner, age 53, has a 15-month-old baby, courtesy of his second wife? Mister Dances-With-Diapers has three grown children from a previous marriage.

I know how he feels. We just got a new dog.

Actually, it's a used dog. We got her from a shelter, which informed us that the prior elderly owners (before us, the current elderly owners) were no longer able to take care of her.

I know how they feel too. Apparently they'd resorted to simply keeping this beagle in her crate most of the time, and overfeeding her out of guilt, thus creating the prototypical American dog: sedentary and morbidly obese.

(By the way, have you noticed how we pet owners say "crate"? A normal person would look at this container of metal bars and call it a cage, but a cage is something you put an animal in, and we don't acknowledge that our pets are animals instead of family members. Thus, we say, "crate," which is also not something you put family members in, as a general rule, but at least it's not a cage. It's complicated.)

So anyway, we bring home this 5-year-old beagle named Ginger, and immediately have to start coping with stuff that we haven't faced in years, either with our kids or with our late lamented beagle Pockets.

Stuff like wastebaskets.

Turns out she's a dumpster-diver, charging head-first into every available trash receptacle that has ever held a food wrapper. The kitchen wastebasket, of course, merits the place of honor, and many's the time we have found her hip-deep in it, with coffee grounds and used kleenex all over the floor.

Reasoning with her on this topic has proven less than productive, thus supporting the well-known description of beagles: all nose, no brain.

Anyway, like Mr. Costner, I'm sure, my husband and I resolved not to make the same mistakes with little Take Two that we had with her predecessors. So, we enrolled the three of us in obedience school. (We weren't sure who'd end up obeying whom, but we liked the 2-to-1 odds.)

Before class started, we had a chat with the instructor, who asked if there were any special problems with Ginger. I brought up the trash issue, hoping that our Zenmaster would have some better idea than putting the wastebasket up on the kitchen counter.

"Have you tried putting the wastebasket up on the kitchen counter?" she inquired. And this is the expert, the one we're paying money to?

Anyway, once class got underway, we discovered that Ginger had a Gandhi-like approach of passive resistance to authority. Rather than learn to sit, stand, heel, etc., she'd simply go limp and sprawl on the floor, refusing to cooperate and inspiring the other dogs to resist as well. I can see how that could bring down an empire.

What else? Let's see. We've trundled Ginger to the vet several times already for minor ailments, the most recent being a sprained tail.

How do you sprain your tail? Wagging too hard? The vet eyed us warily as she examined the dog (reminding me, come to think of it, of the way the pediatrician used to look at us when we'd bring one of the kids in with some oddball injury. You'd be surprised how difficult it is to explain why your kid was handcuffed when she tripped and fell down the stairs.)

Fortunately, there's no DCFS equivalent for pets, so the vet just cautioned us against roughhousing with the dog for a few days. Ginger smirked at us all the way home, assuming (since she has a brain the size of a walnut) that this meant no obedience school that week.

Ha! You'll have to do better than spraining your tail, my little pretty. We've paid good money for this class, and by God you're going. Don't you roll your eyes at me, princess. I'm your mother: you show me some respect.

Anyway, that's our story. Now, if you'll excuse me, I have some dog vomit to clean up. Lord, I'm getting too old for this. How does Kevin Costner do it?

Things did not work out well with Ginger. Let's just let it go at that.

Boogie Woogie Beagle Boys
July 20, 2009

Need something else to make you feel inadequate? How about your dog? I read a newspaper article recently about dogs who are trained to assist people with mental or emotional problems: Seeing Eye dogs for the mind. These dogs are trained to recognize changes in a person's respiration or scent that indicate the person is about to have a panic attack, and to calm the person down.

I looked over at our two twin 7-year-old beagles, both snoring loudly, one sprawled on the living room couch, the other curled contentedly on one of what used to be our nice living room chairs. Sense a panic attack? These guys couldn't sense a nuclear attack. I sighed and continued reading.

The super dogs, it seems, are usually Labs or golden retrievers, the intellectual royalty of the canine world. Beagles, in contrast, are the mental lightweights, requiring much more repetition than the average dog in learning even simple commands. That was what was so astounding about a beagle winning Best in Show in 2008; dog experts were stunned that a beagle could be trained to do anything. (My husband insists that I differentiate between intelligence and trainability. He's right. Beagles are very smart about getting exactly what they want, which is more food.)

Back to the article, where one retriever, named Tuesday, was described as having been trained to awaken his master from crippling nightmares. Hey, our beagle boys can go him one better. Not only will they awaken us from crippling nightmares; they will awaken us from pretty much any kind of sleep, sound or otherwise, if they (a) are hungry, (b) need to be let out, (c) are themselves having crippling nightmares, or (d) just feel like it.

Again, I couldn't help but contrast the noble golden retriever in the article -- who reminds his master, a war vet suffering from post-traumatic stress disorder, to take his prescribed medication -- with the twin cuties who rule our roost. Our guys do little of any usefulness whatsoever, other than to look adorable. Occasionally one of them vomits, just to let us know he's still alive. The spewer is also a coprophage. Look it up. It does give you a strong incentive to keep the yard all picked up.

Sometimes, for no particular reason, our beagles leap up and start going after each other ferociously, chasing, wrestling, biting, after which they resume getting along fine. Parents of boys tell us that this is completely normal. We only had daughters, so our experience was limited to witnessing stomping up stairs, slammed doors, and silent treatments, none of which our dogs have engaged in. Yet.

These unpredictable dogfights, though, are a bit unnerving. The animal shelter where we found our guys a few months ago convinced us to take both of them instead of just one, pleading that the two brothers had never been apart and would probably suffer severe separation anxiety if they were split up. Misty-eyed, we agreed to the two-fer. They'd never been apart, people! What God had put together, we sure as heck weren't going to rend asunder.

After a week or so in our home, however, the boys started their dogfight incidents, and we began to speculate: what if these brothers had spent seven years cooped up with each other, hating each other, and being put up for adoption in a shelter was their first opportunity to get away from each other? What if Fate had led us to that shelter precisely so that we could rend them asunder . . . and we had blown it?

Oh well, it wouldn't be the first time. I continued reading. Tuesday the Perfect Golden Retriever can, allegedly, respond to 82 commands, mostly oriented toward helping physically handicapped people. These commands include turning on lights with his nose, retrieving food off of shelves, and (get this) helping load the washing machine. Are you thinking what I'm thinking?

Is this dog single?

Ain't Nuthin' But Hound Dogs
March 3, 2010

So I was at the bank the other day, taking out a third mortgage on the house in order to pay the staggering veterinary bills on our adorable twin 8-year-old beagles, when our daughter suggested that perhaps the dogs had Munchausen Syndrome.

You've heard of Munchausen's, right? That's a mental disorder in which you self-induce symptoms in order to get people to pay attention to you. Now, a kid faking a cough in order to stay home from school does not have Munchausen's: he's normal. A person inventing a medical problem in order to file or win a lawsuit does not have Munchausen's; he's an American.

Anyway, I began pondering whether our dogs might have Munchausen's, so I Googled "canine Munchausen's Syndrome." Well, apparently ours is a case of first impression, as the lawyers say, because there was nothing about dogs inflicting illnesses on themselves for attention.

Why would our little hounds bring on all of these maladies? The food allergies, the thyroid deficiency, the floating kneecap, eating the mouse poison, needing two teeth pulled, the coprophagy, the abscess in the anal gland, the heart murmur, the intestinal parasite: were these all just products of their fevered imaginations and their desperate need for attention? Were they doing this to each other, in an orgy of mutual Munchausen's?

We needed answers. And we needed money, because these boys were driving us to the poorhouse, or the doghouse.

First, we tried reasoning with them. We spread the vet bills out on the floor; you can guess what the dogs did to them. OK, maybe budgeting is not their long suit. We tried talking to them in simple terms; they fell asleep, deliberately snoring loudly and twitching their legs to make sure we understood that they were dreaming about chasing squirrels, not about working out a payment plan with the vet.

Clearly, their psychological problems were too deep for the rational part of their minds to fathom. Reasoning with beagles, by the way, is not that successful even in the best of circumstances. They're not called "all nose, no brain" for nothing.

So we upped the ante. We went for the beaglecam, hoping to catch them in the act when they were alone in the house: plotting, leafing through medical dictionaries for ideas, swallowing food coloring, etc. Instead, we got nothing.

When we're gone, they sleep. They don't plot. They don't police the perimeter to check for prowlers (not that we thought they would, but still . . .). Once in a great while, they wake up, jump down from the couch/bed/chair, get a drink of water, return to the c/b/c, and go back to sleep.

How on earth can they sleep so many hours? I know you don't expect much from creatures with brains the size of a walnut, but honestly! Then we thought maybe they were jimmying with the video recording equipment, like in the movies where the security guards are watching the video monitor, believing that it's a live feed when it's not, and meanwhile somebody's robbing the vault or stealing the painting.

That's certainly a possibility, although it seems unlikely, since these are the same dogs who lack the mental skills to unwrap their leashes when they're around a tree. "Problem solving!" we plead with them, as they strain mightily, pulling in the wrong direction. Finally we sigh, tromp through the snow over to the tree, walk them back, and then watch as they gallop madly, tongues flying, toward and around the next obstacle they can find: tree, lamp post, yard sign, elderly pedestrian. The neighbor's German shepherd looks out the window at them with contempt. "Schweinhunden!" he thinks to himself, and returns to watching C-Span.

Once, we were able to turn our dogs loose in a large open field in rural Michigan. They charged at top speed toward each other from opposite ends, and at the last minute . . . no, neither of them turned aside. They collided, then got up and scampered off, smiling broadly. How has their breed survived this long?

At any rate, we're stumped about their numerous maladies. And don't be bringing up Munchausen's-by-proxy, because, believe me, we don't need this kind of attention. Plus, I don't know how to induce an anal gland abscess. Really. I don't.

So don't ask.

Section 3: Travel And Adventure

Road Trip!
January 3, 2008

"Hurry up and get in the car, kids. We need to put in a hundred miles before breakfast."

Do those words bring on shudders, a nameless dread, or, worst of all, the sensation of having a full bladder and not being able to do anything about it? If so, my bet is that you were raised by Trip Nazis.

I know I was. Years of my childhood were spent huddled in the back seats of un-air-conditioned cars, legs contorted around the food container -- referred to by my mother as the "Scotch cooler," not because it held Scotch (at least I don't think it did), and certainly not because it cooled anything, but because its aluminum exterior bore the sturdy Scotch tartan then favored by its manufacturer, the 3M Company, also makers of Scotch tape.

We had a food container in the car because we weren't the kind of family that could just stop and buy a meal whenever they got hungry. That kind of family probably burned $100 bills for fuel too. No, we brought our own food along on a trip: grapes, apples, peanut butter and jelly sandwiches. Those are foods whose flavor does not improve after sitting for hours in a big can in a warm car, let me tell you. Just ask your kids how their lunches taste after marinating in their lockers all morning.

On the other hand, in those pre-fast-food days, you were probably rolling the dice if you pulled into any old roadside diner. Local color is one thing, but not if you're going to lose it all over the back seat an hour after you're back on the road.

Thus the first hallmark of Trip Nazis is, bring your own food. The second is, no stopping, ever, for anything, except to buy more 29-cent per gallon gas for your 10-mpg roadster with its 25-gallon fuel tank. My family took a lot of trips between California and Missouri, so we passed by a lot of souvenir shops in the great southwest with cool-looking feathered tomahawks and beaded moccasins in the windows. Did we ever stop? Do I sound as if we ever stopped? No and no.

Forget any shopping excursions; even bathroom stops were strongly discouraged, both because they were time bandits and because the restroom facilities were of uncertain quality. Eating on the road may have been rolling the dice; relieving yourself on the road was more akin to Russian roulette. You just had to make sure your tank was in opposite sync with the car's tank: when it was full, yours had better be empty. That's why you didn't read about any drinks in the Scotch cooler three paragraphs ago: if we were thirsty, we ate grapes.

The third sure-fire trait of Trip Nazis was, they smoked in the car. My own kids are horrified by this: "Grandma and Grandad did that to you?" I nod nonchalantly, explaining, as we do so often, "Things were different then." And they WERE different, both because of the smoking, and because it simply was not a child-centered universe. So the kids were uncomfortable: so what? For my kids, who put the DCFS hotline number on our speed dial as soon as their chubby little fingers could operate a phone, my parents' outlook was incomprehensible, almost pre-Copernican.

Interestingly, my husband turns out to have had childhood experiences similar to mine, with a slightly different twist on account of his having Greek-American parents who insisted on bringing dolmades, spanikopita, feta cheese and olives in the Scotch cooler. The Trip Nazi gene expresses itself differently in different families, but it's still there.

To be continued ...

Once again Sally Sotos was unable to confine herself to the space limitation generously provided her. So, put this on the refrigerator next to the Bed, Bath and Beyond coupon of the week, and wait for her sequel. And wait. And wait ...

Road Trip!, Part Duh
January 9, 2008

As I was saying . . .

On the cross-country trips of his youth, my husband wasn't drawn to souvenir shops on the road, as I was. Instead, he and his brother clamored for a glimpse of the freak show tourist traps whose billboards boasted of defying the laws of nature: places where gravity didn't work, where plumb lines hung sideways, where the diameter of a circle was smaller than its radius. His Greek immigrant parents were having none of it. They were immune to the siren song of American roadside life.

And where, you may ask, did our wacky, but not Kerouac-y, families spend the night while On The Road? At a Holiday Inn or a Howard Johnson Motor Lodge ("HoJoMoLo" to those in the know)? Ha! Why not suggest the Ritz while you're at it?

No, your first option was to find some distant member of the family who lived en route, and bunk with them for free. We didn't have any relatives between Phoenix and Salina, however, so we stayed in places that looked like . . . well, like the Bates Motel.

(See, the younger generation nowadays doesn't understand that one of the reasons *Psycho* was scary was not that the motel looked so creepy; the movie was scary because in 1960 the motel looked so normal. A lot of motels looked like the Bates back then.)

Places like the Bates had interesting, now-obsolete items in the rooms like coin-operated TV, pay radio, and Magic Fingers vibrating beds: ups and extras that, we kids assumed, were used freely by the fabulously wealthy people who customarily spent the night there. Our parents, of course, never paid the outrageous user fees (25 cents a pop, I think) for these novelty gadgets.

We'd spend a restless night (kids on rollaway cots, parents on the saggy double bed) and then be up and away at dawn. It was a crappy way to travel, truth be told, but we weren't made of money, as our parents frequently reminded us. No wonder our generation spends money like drunken sailors on shore leave: we have years of childhood privation to make up for.

So, anyway, when my husband and I got to sit in the front seat of life and plan the family trip how we wanted, we vowed not to repeat our parents' ways. "It's the journey, not the destination, kids," we'd say, as we meandered along the by-ways of the Midwest. Unfortunately, when you have little kids in the back seat, it IS the destination, not the journey, believe me. "Are we there yet?" (the rallying cry of back-seaters across the nation) is not easily answered with existential ponderings like, "That depends on your definition of 'there,' sweetie," or "We're always there."

As we've gotten older, and our travels no longer include the kids, we really do do it Our Way. We take potty stops and lumbar back stretch stops every 90 minutes, so that a 400-mile trip to Minnesota takes approximately a day and a half.

The ultimate irony, of course, is that the Trip Nazi gene is a generation-skipping gene. Having suffered through interminable trips to nowhere, our kids are ferocious Trip Nazis (well, except for the smoking part). I personally observed our older daughter instructing her boyfriend to stop drinking water two hours before their scheduled departure time, warning him that there would be no stops.

He's a nice kid, so I pulled him aside. "She can't help it," I explained. "She was raised by hoboes and vagabonds." He nodded understandingly: "That's what she says." He smiled politely, and finished his water bottle. Turning to our daughter, he asked, "What else should we put in the cooler beside oranges and Clif bars? How about some trail mix?"

I shook my head. You can't fight the gene pool.

Benz Me, Shape Me
July 23, 2008

So we got this new car (new to us, I mean; built when Ronald Reagan was in his first term) just when gas was hitting $3 a gallon. Remember $3 a gallon? The good old days?

It's a cute little roadster, and we got it for a song. Unfortunately, the song was, "It's Too Late, Baby." We should have bought it 10 years, or 10,000 miles, ago, when our hearts were young and our bodies weren't pooling at the joints yet.

But back then, we needed a car that could haul kids to soccer practice, and bring home big stuff from the lumber yard, and carry a week's worth of groceries at one time. (Like the true European it is, our snappy roadster is more comfortable with the concept of daily food shopping.)

Instead, we waited until we were too old for this sort of thing. What do I mean? Well, this car is not built for comfort. When you're in it, your rear end is lower than your knees, so bystanders gather around to gawk when you try and struggle out of it. My husband -- the one with the bum knee and the hip replacement -- has finally figured out a way to accordian-pleat himself in and out with a minimum of wincing, but there is still only an inch of clearance between the bottom of the steering wheel and the top of the driver's thigh.

I thought Germans were design wizards! Maybe this is their post-war revenge. The Soviets said, "We will bury you;" the Germans say, "We will make your sciatica act up again."

The shoulder strap part of the seat belt was not designed for my build -- well, what is, really? -- and exerts constant pressure on my shoulder joint, the one with the ongoing rotator cuff problem. Luckily, I've discovered that a potholder folded just right will cushion the strap, if worn on the shoulder like an epaulet. Very practical and, depending on your selection of potholders, kind of stylish.

Bottom line: even with the sun roof open, the windows down and the radio set on WNUA, it's tough to maintain the delusion that you're a slightly older version of the Girl From Ipanema with a potholder on your shoulder, your reading glasses on a chain around your neck, your regular glasses (with the clip-on sun shades) slipping off your nose, and your well-worn lumbar back support pad in place, while you're rushing to the pharmacy to pick up your bladder control medicine.

    Not that I would know, of course . . .

Spring Break 2K8!
April 16, 2008

"This is what Patton meant: no break in the cloud cover for a bombing run," my husband observed, peering up at the bleak Belgian sky. We were in Brussels for a week in late March, visiting our older daughter. The gods of Travel and Tourism were obviously angry with us: how else to explain the perfect storm of (1) terrible exchange rates, (2) unseasonably rotten weather, and (3) a sudden outbreak of foot and knee injuries in the family? I'd call us the walking wounded, but "walking" is an overly kind description of the hobbling, wincing, grumbling way we travelled.

But, hey, we had made it to Europe! Our younger daughter sacrificed her spring vacation to join us, and decided to fill any conversational pauses by demonstrating what she had been learning in her self-defense class at college, so that she would periodically urge, "Grab my wrist," the way she used to say, "Pull my finger." The younger ones are always the class clowns, aren't they?

Now, some of you may envision Europe as portrayed in forty-year-old pictures from your high school French book, depicting folks with their sweaters tied around their shoulders in a way that would get you beaten up in America. Well, news flash: we saw almost no one with their sweaters that way, so you can quit practicing that loose square knot.

Instead, everyone wears gorgeous scarves draped casually around the neck. Don't bother trying to achieve that look with your scarf. You'll never look as cool as they do. You know it, and they know it. Move ahead.

Other observations about clothing: apparently, it is not cool for the natives to wear hats, mittens, gloves, or even coats (scarves are always mandatory, of course), although the weather was cold, raining, snowing, and hailing. Simultaneously. In fact, the restaurants were setting up their outdoor sidewalk tables and chairs for some al fresco dining. Go figure.

You can always spot the Americans a mile away, because they are actually dressed for cold weather, and because they smile. The Belgians exhibit only their Euroface, a combination of glum and tragic. Looking at the exchange rate, we wondered what THEY had to complain about. Plus, they all dress in dark clothing, so that sometimes you feel you've stumbled into a Johnny Cash fan club convention.

Speaking of restaurants, they're everywhere. Maybe the natives figure, why bother going to the trouble of cooking at home, when you can go someplace right down the street and get the best bread / pastries / waffles / whatever on the PLANET? (Here in the States, that attitude sends people by the busload to Old Country Buffet. Hmm...)

And, yes, in Belgium, they do serve waffles - Belgian waffles - from little wagons located on every block. We saw no wagons serving Brussels sprouts: can you imagine?

You do need to prepare yourself for the fact that they serve their French fries (which they call Belgian fries) with... mayonaise. You can ask for ketchup, if you want to have big Bozo arrows pointing at you and flashing, "I'M NOT FROM THESE PARTS." Don't do that. They worked hard getting that mayo to taste just right.

The point is, the food is fabulous. Not that the American Airlines airplane food on the flight over wasn't great too, of course. Actually, my main complaint about that particular experience was one of timing: when you serve food and drink to hundreds of people simultaneously, you should expect that they will be in gastro-synchronous digestive orbit, with the inevitable rush on flush. Memo to airline: install more lavatories. Now.

Speaking of which, we did get to experience, in Europe, one of the truly fine innovations which we in the States really should emulate: the toilets, which have two different kinds of flushes to choose from, a #1 level and a #2 level, so to speak. Why doesn't Al Gore talk this up? It involves water conservation, AND it's an issue everyone could be pro-choice about! Win-Win!

Gosh, there's so much more to tell you about, but apparently the higher-ups at the Independent want you to wait for it. So, stay tuned for the next instalment, covering European Elevators (Size Does Matter); Madame Sotos, Your Papers Are Not In Order; and other heart-stoppers.

Over There, Part Deux
April 23, 2008

    Our walking tour of Brussels, with side trips to Paris and Bruges, was hampered somewhat by the torn miniscuses and sprained ankles we had managed to come down (literally) with the week before. But we weren't deterred: we had powerful painkilling drugs, enabling us to exacerbate our injuries without feeling any discomfort in the process. Hurray, Big Pharma!

    We would caution you, though: as you stroll (or, in our case, limp) around the cobblestone streets and sidewalks, craning your neck upward to admire the gorgeous architecture, don't forget that all Belgians own dogs, and no Belgians pick up after their dogs, so that the sidewalks are dangerous. The British say, "Mind the gap;" the Belgians should say, "Mind the cr--."

    You should also bear in mind that, since a lot of the buildings in Europe are super-old, elevators were shoe-horned in as an afterthought, and are thus unbelievably small. We actually got down and measured the floor of the elevator in the building we stayed in: it was a square meter (translation: 39" by 39"). You tape that off on the kitchen floor and see how you'd like getting up close and personal with strangers that way.

    On the other hand, many escalators are designed to be activated by your approach: they don't run continuously. This probably saves energy, and also gives your spirits a boost, because you look at the escalator and think it's out of order (darn!), then, as if reading your thoughts, it springs into action (yay!).

    Speaking of not being in order, we did have one unnerving experience while on the super-speedy train from Brussels to Paris. The train conductor, from the Flemish branch of the Belgian populace, rather than the French branch (think Hatfields and McCoys, Montagues and Capulets, Jewel and Dominick's), scrutinized our tickets and then announced, in rather Teutonic-accented English, that our papers were not in order.

    He actually said that, people. We had trouble keeping from

giggling, until we realized he was serious and would probably throw us off the super-speedy train with no compunction, while it was moving. Everything got straightened out eventually, of course; turns out we had grabbed our kids' youth-rate tickets instead of our senior-level ones. The conductor probably had trouble keeping from giggling when he saw that: "How stupid do zeez old Americans sink we are?"

We spent only a day in Paris, which is ridiculous, of course, particularly since it happened to be the day that the French and English national soccer teams had an exhibition match, what they call a "friendly," in Paris. Friendly was not what I would call the crowds of drunken British fans that began milling and drinking outside the restaurants and bars around our train station in Paris. We got the distinct impression that these folks had not grown up playing AYSO. Fortunately, the gendarmes soon arrived and dispersed the mob, so that the Sotos family, their papers now in order, could catch the Super-Speedy back to Brussels.

What else can I tell you about Europe? Let's see: don't expect to walk around town jauntily with a giant cup of coffee in your hand, as you do in the States. These folks don't believe in take-out coffee. Sit down and drink it here, mon ami. In contrast, the place next to our apartment building in Brussels was a combination sushi take-out / convenience store, where we could buy wine, Ben and Jerry's, and sushi to go: not a bad combo, actually.

We'd grab the essentials at the end of a long day of limping, and head up to our flat, where we relaxed by watching Belgian TV. The most fascinating program there was an infomercial for Juke Box Memories CD's, with the American songs from the '50's left intact but the interviews with misty-eyed American Baby Boomers dubbed in French. Let me tell you, there's not enough Pinot Noir and Chunky Monkey in Belgium to get you through that experience without some projectile laughing.

Europe was fabulous, of course, but it made me slightly melancholy, as I remembered that I had turned sixteen in Paris, on spring break of my junior year in high school. Then, I was the one handling things in French for my parents. This time, our older daughter was running interference for us in French. I turned fifty-five the day we got back home, and felt old. Where's my Vicodin?

In case you ever wondered, sirens in Europe really do have that two-note, sing-song sound. It's cute.

All Aboard!
February 4, 2009

Who's up for a big ol' bus trip? I know, I know: you swore off traveling long distances by bus years ago, back when the Greyhound station was right smack in the middle of the Loop; back when the bus clientele did not reflect the sort of folks you aspired to hang out with; back when you learned a lot about life from walking through the bus station; back when you developed the ability to hold it (as in, oh-my-aching-urethra) for Guinness-record-breaking periods of time, because ainnoway you'd use a Greyhound bathroom.

In other words, The Good Old Days.

Forget 'em! Say hello to the Megabus, maybe the most serious competition the 'Hound has faced since Trailways. Actually, I have no idea if that's true, but here's the point: I know people who have taken the Megabus and lived to tell the tale!

Maybe you're like my husband, whose memories of bus rides include field trips from the military academy he attended as a youth (or do you say "yute"?). The first leg of the field trip would include full-throated renditions of those immortal travel tunes, "99 Bottles of Beer" and "Hand Jive," repeated until the faculty chaperones -- combat-hardened veterans of the Battle of the Bulge, the Bataan Death March and the invasion of Inchon -- were reduced to quivering mounds of jelly, ready to confess to war crimes they had never witnessed or even contemplated.

Once the adults on the bus were effectively neutralized, the boys could get about the real business of the trip, springing for each others' throats. My husband still thinks *Lord of the Flies* was a documentary.

Anyway, back to the bus. The first thing you'll notice about the Megabus trip is that it's incredibly cheap: alarmingly, jaw-droppingly, how-can-they-do-it-that-cheaply, cheap. Even with low, low gas prices, you can't drive this cheaply, and you certainly can't fly or train. Maybe you could thumb it for less, but haven't we outgrown that phase?

There are a couple of reasons why taking the Megabus is so inexpensive. First: no overhead. Literally. There is no Megabus station. I don't mean it's like Platform 9 3/4 of the Hogwarts Express; I mean there's no station, period, anywhere. Megabus relies on the kindness of strangers.

In Chicago, one of those strangers is Union Station: the bus stop is described on the Megabus website as "east side of Canal Street, about 300 feet south of Jackson Blvd." The bus pulls up; the driver alights, places a sturdy wooden sign reading "Megabus!" on the sidewalk, and voila! Like J.K. Rowling's Knight Bus. There's your DIY bus stop: a step above, but not far above, that one in the middle of nowhere in *North by Northwest*, where Cary Grant gets dumped off right before the cropduster starts buzzing him.

We conjecture that another reason for the Megabus' low fares may be that each trip appears to be underwritten by a different fast food chain. The Minneapolis-Chicago run seems brought to you by Subway, while the good folks at Hardee's may be subsidizing the Ann Arbor-Chicago trip. At least, that would be the logical explanation for the 9 a.m. "lunch" stops the bus makes. Ah, the romance of travel.

Right about now, you're probably asking yourself, "Who rides the Megabus?" (Actually, you're really asking yourself, "Are the Obamas about the most perfect-looking family you've ever seen? Why can't my family look that perfect?" I understand. My family is tired of hearing me note that Michelle and I are both lawyers, both married to lawyers, both 5'11", both mother of two daughters, and yet somehow I am nowhere near her in coolness. Clearly my family is holding me back, keeping me down. That coulda been me at the Inaugural Ball. I coulda been a contender. Grr. Forget it: try and focus on the Megabus.)

So, who rides the Megabus? Definitely a higher quality of vagabonds and nomads than in days of yore, for the simple reason that the only way to book a trip on the Megabus is online. Thus, anyone who lacks access to, or the skills to navigate on, the Interweb, is not Megabus material. Keeps out riff-raff like me, that's for sure.

Anyway, next time you need to travel to a faraway spot, leave that car in the garage. Sure, the car is convenient, and private, and you won't have to borrow someone else's wheels once you get to your destination, but those are minor considerations. Mass transit is the way of the future, so get on board before that train leaves the station!

So to speak.

Sally Sotos thanks journalist Jim Lileks for his colorful description of holding it.

Not Another Road Trip!
March 25, 2009

They say that traveling together brings a family closer.
Closer to counseling, maybe.
That's our conclusion after our most recent road trip, this time, to Washington, D.C., where our older daughter landed her dream job with an environmental policy think tank. Different people have different dreams, I guess. Anyway, we were along to be her wingmen while she went apartment-hunting.

First, though, we had to get there with her stuff, which meant we had to drive her there and then drive her car back, since apparently no one in their right mind owns a car in Washington, as there is no place to put it (perhaps an early example of federal bureaucratic planning).

Now, when I say we brought our daughter's "stuff," I mean we filled up the spacious trunk of her 1996 Lincoln as well as our little 1967 (yes, you're reading that right) trailer, named Old Blue for obvious reasons. At one time, possibly when LBJ was president, it had been painted bright blue, but now rust, primer and chipped blue paint elbowed each other for position on its sad body.

The sturdy top of the trailer had given up the ghost over the winter, and we had meant to get a new one (really, we had), but time got away from us, so in lieu of a top you could lock, we used old carpet remnants and a large plastic tarpaulin, lashed down with hauling chains.

We thus entered our nation's capital looking like something out of The Grapes of Wrath, or maybe "The Beverly Hillbillies." Needless to say, our daughter wore a bag over her head, perhaps worried that Barack and Michelle would be out strolling down Pennsylvania Avenue with the kids just as we came rolling into town, and would point at us and say, "Look at those rubes with the Illinois plates. Hey, isn't that the Sotos family? Let us mock them."

However, I get ahead of myself. First, we had to get there. Our daughter had made all the arrangements on-line, of course, and informed us that Google pegged the trip at 12-14 hours. But we are not Googlicious drivers: we need stretch breaks and potty breaks and sciatica breaks; plus, 8-9 hours is about our max, so we overnighted in Pittsburgh, and then finished the journey the next day: from our front door to Courtyard Inn's front door in D.C., about 26 hours. Hey, in life, you need to make time to stop and smell the asphalt.

Complicating the trip was the driver situation. Our daughter slept most of the way, so she was essentially useless behind the wheel. My husband had been nursing a sinus infection which had somehow migrated into his eye; the only relief he could get was from strong antihistamines and decongestants, so he had to strike a delicate balance between drying out and passing out. I called him Bad-Eye Moody.

That left me, but unfortunately, among the many anxieties I have acquired over the years -- like barnacles on the side of a ship -- are ones involving heights and edges and elevated roadways, things that the Pennsylvania Turnpike specializes in. So I spent a fair amount of time in a state of quivering panic, praying, "Please, Lord, I promise I will build a great cathedral in Your honor if I can just get through southwestern Pennsylvania without shrieking or sobbing or vomiting or soiling myself."

Let's just say I won't be taking out a building permit anytime soon.

In any event, we finally arrived. You know how the car gets by the end of a trip: you're ankle-deep in empty styrofoam cups, dried-up tea bags, apple cores, banana peels, crossword puzzles, maps, used kleenex, empty pop bottles, receipts, crushed juice boxes, half-empty mustard packets and one glove. The interior of the car smells foul. YOU smell foul.

Still ... we had made it! My husband emerged from the car with driver's limp, while holding one hand over his sore eye, so he bore a passing resemblance to Long John Silver. But instead of a hearty "Aarrggh," he complained, "I tried to wire ahead that we were coming, but did you know that you can't send a telegram anymore? When the hell did that happen?"

To be continued ...

Road Trip to D.C.
April 1, 2009

(This is the second column detailing a trip to our nation's capital to move our older daughter. If you didn't catch the first one, don't worry, you didn't miss much.)

As we limped through the motel doors on March 14, we immediately knew we weren't in Kansas anymore, so to speak: the lobby was filled with Japanese high school students wearing St. Patrick's Day regalia: shamrock necklaces, tall green-and-white-striped Cat in the Hat hats, "Kiss Me I'm Irish" T-shirts. We wanted to take a picture of them, but refrained out of political correctness.

They were perhaps thinking the same thing about us: we had loaded up the motel's rolling luggage cart with our bags, pillows, backpacks, maps and coolers, so we probably looked like peasants on the Trans-Siberian Railroad, minus the cages of squawking chickens. We strolled to the check-in desk with as much dignity as we could muster. The desk clerk eyed us and our cart and sighed, as if remembering the days when the place had attracted a better class of guests. We didn't help our cause by immediately trying to present all the membership discounts we could. AAA? AARP? YMCA? Jewel check-cashing card?

We were eventually ensconced in our room, and my husband had to admit that our daughter's on-line arrangements had worked out better than his usual travel plan, which was to roll into town and then drive around looking for a neon Vacancy sign. It was in his DNA, I think: his father apparently had a similar practice on family trips, namely, drive until you run out of food in the car and the kids have gnawed all the oranges down to the peel, then cruise around until you find the local Greek restaurant, go in and talk to the owner about the old country.

(Of course, it's hard to know what to believe about your spouse's childhood tales. My husband also swears that his grandmother buried her jewelry in a box in the backyard, to keep it from the gypsies or the Turks. Actually, that one rang a bell, as my own

Nebraska grandmother had allegedly often expressed to her children her worry that they would be kidnapped by gypsies. That's Omaha, all right: Gateway to Gypsy Country.)

    Back to D.C., where driving around, apartment-hunting, is no easy matter. First, the place was platted by European urban planners, so guess what? No provision for vehicles; 15-foot-wide residential lots; no grid layout for the streets; and an address system which makes delivering the mail or, in our case, locating a building, critically dependent on specifying what quadrant of town you're looking for. It's thus a very European city: can't drive in it, expensive, impractical and beautiful.

    So we checked out about a half dozen apartments, most of which provoked my husband into exclamations about the high cost of everything. "Don't scratch your budget in public," I murmured, elbowing him in the ribs. Thankfully, our daughter managed to snag the best-looking apartment in the safest location, in her price range. Thank you, Lord. Once again I promise to build a great cathedral in Your honor . . . or perhaps You would settle for a small chapel? How about an upright bathtub in the backyard?

    All too soon, my husband and I were on our way, retracing our route back to Illinois, once again encountering the eternal bane of every highway traveller, namely, having all traffic narrowed to one lane by miles of orange cones, with no sign of any work actually being done, except by the guys who are putting up and taking down the cones. Misty-eyed, I recalled our daughter's parting words. Mindful that she had been the fodder of many of these columns, she smirked, "You won't have Mary Sotos to kick around anymore!"

    That's what you think, sister.

You Think YOU Had A Bad Trip!
December 30, 2009

Last week our older daughter complained that, prior to her recent flight out of Washington, D.C., the plane sat on the tarmac for an hour and a half before taking off. Next to her was a mom with a 6-month-old baby who spent the ninety minutes expressing his views on the delay at the top of his lungs.

Boo hoo. That's why God invented I-Pods. MY candidate for Worst Airplane Trip Ever was one I read about in the paper last spring. Like most newspaper stories, however, it raised more questions than it answered.

Seems that there was this Russian-born lady, described by the press as a "British artist, actress and author who rubs elbows with the rich and famous." She had flown from London to Los Angeles to have a face-to-face with a guy she'd met over the Internet.

Now, we haven't even gotten to the meat of the story, and already you're thinking, "artist, actress and author"? Is that code for "unemployed groupie"? How exactly do you "rub elbows" with someone? Where did that expression come from? And if she's hanging out with glamourous British people, why does she have to fly halfway around the world to meet someone? And how can an unemployed groupie afford the air fare?

Let's continue with this already-under-researched story. It's not clear what happened on the Internet blind date, but our British Russkie must have gotten homesick for Big Ben, because she soon hopped a flight back to London. Somewhere in there, though, she realized that she had the dreaded Fear of Flying.

(Here, I can empathize, having spent several years of my life with a F.of F. It started when my kids were young, and has begun to dissipate now that they are of an age to survive without me advising them when to take an umbrella, when to take a cab home, etc. Once you realize your kids don't really need you anymore, your subconscious goes into "what the heck, why not" mode, and your F. of F. goes out the window. At high altitudes.)

Anyway, Ms. Minsk took the self-medicating route: according to the newspaper story, she took "4 sleeping pills and consumed two or three bottles of red wine to calm her nerves," all while still over American soil.

Again, questions, questions: does this sound like something you do to calm your nerves -- or to blot out the memory of a really bad date, one you had flown 8,000 miles for, only to discover that Mr. Right did not exactly match his on-line description of himself? This is how you wasted the last of your frequent flyer miles, when you could have been rubbing elbows with Jude Law or that guy who voices the Geico gecko? My guess is, the four sleeping pills and two or three bottles of wine were just an appetizer.

Somewhere over the Midwest, our heroine was found with her feet on the food tray, kicking the seat in front of her. (Just about now, you're thinking that you've been on a flight with this gal yourself, right?) A short time later, she was observed drinking a bottle of liquid soap from the bathroom and complaining about the quality of the airline's red wine. She then fell to the floor, began snapping like a dog, and tried to bite a stewardess' leg.

People, I don't make this stuff up; I only report it. But again, we're missing the key details. Drinking liquid soap to try to kill the taste of the cabernet seems drastic, but with all the cutbacks in airline service, maybe it was necessary. United's house brand ("Ted's Red") is probably not an award winner.

More importantly, however, the implication is that she consumed the two or three bottles of wine ON BOARD. How was she permitted to be so over-served? Do you think the flight crew cut her some slack on account of the expensive bad date in L.A., or on account of the elbow-rubbing with the British VIPs, or what? Do you think they'd let YOU get snockered at 35,000 feet?

Anyway, the plane had to make an emergency landing at Bangor, Maine (What other kind of landing would there be in Bangor?): the pilot wanted to dump Anastasia off with the feds on the ground, so that he could have a less traumatic trans-Atlantic crossing. Understandable.

The newspaper article concluded that she could face up to a 6-month prison term, but a little sleuthing on my part disclosed

. . . The Rest Of The Story. Unable to post bond (where are those fair-weather rich-and-famous elbow-rubbers when you need a few bucks?), Ms. Rusanova enjoyed the hospitality of the Mainiacs at the Pepperidge Farm Prison (OK, I made that one up) for a few days, and then pled guilty to assault. She got off with time served.

So ends our little Tale of the Bad Trip. Have a happy new year, and lay off the booze for awhile. It can lead to harder stuff. Like liquid soap.

Sally Sotos' New Year's Resolution is that 2010 will be the year she publishes her columns in book form! E-mail her at elmhurstss@aol.com if you think it's a good idea.

Hearing Voices?
March 31, 2010

So we finally joined the rest of the civilized world, and got one of those GPS things for the car. At last! No more dealing with big old paper road maps, where the route you want to take always falls along a worn fold line in the map, and when you point this out to the driver, your finger jabs all the way through the map, creating a large crater on the interstate. Oops.

Forget all that! Now we're ridin' high. Of course, the learning curve is steep at first, triggering the swearfest that so often accompanies the programming of a new device. But once you're past that part, you're in tall cotton.

Now there's someone else in the car with you: a disembodied voice, delivering precise directions uncluttered by trivia or small talk. Instead of a human navigator who gets distracted and confused and spills coffee on the Shell road map with the hole in it and then berates you for taking the wrong turn, you have . . . The Voice.

The worst The Voice ever says is, "Recalculating." No sighs or reproaches. Her silence is not The Silent Treatment, fraught with meaning. It's just silence. I say "her" silence, but you could make it a male voice if you wanted. I prefer the female voice right now, because who needs another man telling you precisely what to do in short, clipped tones? My husband also prefers the female voice: with a wife and two daughters, he's spent decades hearing (and ignoring) women telling him how to drive: what's one more?

I do think the smarty-pants inventors of these gadgets could go a bit further in the voice department, though. Right now, The Voice can speak in several languages (BTW, you may think you can speak French, but try listening, comprehending, and executing instructions while driving in French, mon ami: tres difficile, n'est-ce pas?) and two genders, but there are many more colors on the human vocal palette.

For instance, why not have several well-known voices available, to match your many moods? They'd be downloadable, like ringtones. If you crave a stern taskmaster voice, you could program Maggie Smith as Professor McGonigle. How about a Barry White-type voice for more mellow times?

You could get the Basic package for each voice, which would just give you, well, the basics, or, for a few dollars more, the Premium package, which would be a bit more ... conversational. Right now I'm thinking of (OK, fantasizing about) a Jeremy Irons/Alan Rickman blend with silky, come-hither tones:

"Luv, you might want to turn left in a hundred feet. By the bye, did I tell you how smashing you look today? It's true, I swear it. Oh, blast, look at that: we missed the turn. My fault, luv. Look here, are you sure you really want to go to this meeting/party/ funeral? I can think of a lot more interesting things we could do. Oh, very well. All right, here you go, darling, I've figured out a better way to get there. Take a left in 200 feet, or, as we say, about 60 meters ..."

Road trip? Oh yeah.

And maybe while they're at it, the smarty-pantses could work on voices for some of our other electronic devices as well:

"Look, luv, why don't you check to see if this fool printer is even plugged into the computer? Off you go, there's a good girl." Or,

"I'm not sure that's quite the way they want you to set the time on this digital clock. Here, let me help. Say, have you lost weight? You look marvelous."

The Digital Divide -- the gap between us electronically challenged boomers and everyone else -- could become a distant memory if the nerd inventors would get working on this idea. We oldsters would become proficient on all these gadgets in a (defibrillated) heartbeat.

So listen up, inventors, because we're the demographic you want. Don't waste your time dreaming up new devices for Generation X or Y or Z. To see us through our golden years, we've saddled them with debt up to their I-Pods: their discretionary spending power is going to be down the bidet before they know it.

Instead, you inventors should think AARP. And ASAP, please, while we can still hear and benefit from those voice-added gadgets of yours. We're not getting any younger, you know.

Just deafer.

Indiana Billboards or Hoosier Daddy?
June 2, 2010

"How was the trip up to Michigan this weekend, Mom?"
"OK, except one of the dogs threw up."
"Eeew! Where!"
"Just outside Michigan City."
"No, I mean, where?"
"In the backseat."
"Which one?"
"We only have one backseat, honey."
"No, I mean, which dog?"
"We're still interviewing the witnesses."

Life's like that sometimes. Now, if it had been two kids in the back, instead of two dogs, we parents could have instantly figured out who the culprit was. For one thing, the non-vomiter would have ratted out her sister immediately with a mighty "Eeew!"; for another, the hurler's face would probably have been a sickly shade of green, and her eyes would have been rolling wildly in her head.

But with dogs, see, it's different. Our first clue was an odd odor, but we ignored it because traveling in a confined space with four middle-aged types (two of us, two of them) tends to produce odd odors even in ideal circumstances.

Finally, we looked to the back seat, and were reminded once again why we never invest in new cars. (Our family policy has always been to buy 'em used, drive 'em into the ground and then push 'em into the Cal Sag Canal late at night. Oh, I suppose you have a better plan? Remember, if you do-nate your car to-day, you're only encouraging hideous advertising songs, and the jingle terrorists will have won.)

So, we look, and there's the evidence -- the recycled kibble -- located between the two suspects, who are both looking back at us as if they hadn't had a thing to do with it: "Why, how'd that get there, Mom? Darned if we know. Is it lunchtime yet?"

Anyway, after that happens, you spend a lot of time staring out the window, as you wend your way through Indiana up to Michigan. At first, you're trying to remember why it seemed like such a good idea to get more dogs after the kids were grown and gone, and you finally had the house (and car) to yourselves. That line of thought goes nowhere, so you start to notice -- really notice -- the roadside scenery. And you keep noticing on the way home too.

    The major eye-catcher, of course, is the billboards about fireworks, but, as with much advertising, they raise more questions than answers. For instance, one of the billboards proclaims that Krazy Kaplan's is open 24 hours. Why would a fireworks store need to be open around the clock? "Honey, it's the middle of the night and the baby won't stop crying. Can you run out and pick up some loud explosive devices? That ought to quiet her down."

    For reasons that defy sound zoning principles, fireworks stores in Indiana are located immediately adjacent to heavily traveled expressways, so if the store blows, it's taking a lot of folks down (or up) with it. On the other hand, there's no obviously good spot to site a Krazy Kaplan's, is there?

    The fireworks billboards advertise, "Buy One, Get Six Free," insulting our common sense (which of course is always in overdrive when we're shopping for fireworks), and proclaim that their products are "Direct From China," a fact we had pretty much taken for granted for the last few thousand years: "Argentine firecracker" has generally been understood to be a figure of speech, not a Fourth of July specialty.

    And the fireworks signs are usually near the personal injury lawyer billboards, for obvious reasons: if you're crazy enough to buy fireworks from a bug-eyed man in a straightjacket, you're probably crazy enough to hire a lawyer who sinks his extra money into billboards instead of books.

    What else can we glean about Indiana from its roadside attractions? Well, somebody was smart enough, early on, to plan the expressway through the lowest, marshiest, least commercially useful tracts; you'd think the cat tail was the state flower. In a spirit of sunny optimism, the "Highlands" apartment complex is located in a marsh; you look down on the Highlands as you drive by.

    "They'll never find me there," my husband always says as we pass the Highlands, forgetting that, since he's told me a hundred times that his safe house when he's on the lam will be in the Highlands, the Highlands will in fact be the first place we look. That's right, buster: we. You're not getting out of this scot-free, pal.

Then of course there are the numerous casino ads, with their hordes of happy gamblers: those folks are winsome, and they're winning, aren't they? But America is the land of diversity: where are the pensioners, the guys with the wheelchairs and oxygen tanks? The folks with the gambling problem whom we're counting on to fund our public schools? And where, oh where, are the losers (or, as we say on Wall Street, the counterparties)? I guess nobody wants to be reminded about them, the real unsung (or is that unstrung?) heroes. You can't spell casino without coins, you know.

All too soon, unfortunately, you must bid farewell to the Hoosier state, and say Yes! to Michigan, whose billboards aren't nearly as exotic. But there's one sign that both states have in common:

"Road Construction Ahead. Expect Long Delays."

Section 4: Beauty, Health And Fashion

This I Can't Make Up
August 13, 2008

Guys, this column is for women only, so you just run along and watch the Speed Channel for awhile. I think it's almost time for "Pinks AllOut," so you go on now.

OK, girls, are they gone? Good. Let's talk make-up. Specifically, let's talk about articles about make-up, like the one I saw recently in a large metropolitan newspaper (no, not this one), entitled, "8 make-up mistakes/ Come on, you know you've made them."

I hate this kind of article! I've hated it since I was in high school! In fact, "8 make-up mistakes" was probably written when I was in high school, reading <u>Glamour</u> and <u>Seventeen</u>, and just gets dredged up and rewritten every seven years for a new crop of anxious readers, in order to make them more anxious and thus more likely to buy the products advertised nearby.

Take "Mistake No.2: Chunky mascara on tips of lashes." The suspiciously well-groomed "celebrity make-up artist" (male), whose secrets of success are offered to us in this article, advises that he "curls lashes and then places, say, a business card behind the top lashes." The article says nothing about removing the business card at any time. In what was probably the 1968 version of this article, I'll bet we were advised to use our dad's business card; now, we can use our own! You've come a long way, baby.

Or, how about "Mistake No.3: Bad batwings at the corners of eyes." Old example: Liz Taylor in "Cleopatra;" new example: Amy Winehouse. The instructions, God bless 'em, are as baffling as ever: "Blend a darker eye shadow at the outer corner of the eye, then place a triangular sponge below it, and swipe diagonally up from the eye to create a clean edge. Finally, accentuate with a little black shadow on an angled eyeshadow brush." Being careful not to clip the side of that business card, of course. So now you have a sponge and a business card perched jauntily at eye level. If this were in the Glamour Do's and Don't's, I'm guessing it'd be a Don't, but maybe I'm out of step.

A sidebar to "8 make-up mistakes" is titled, "Mauve's moment," and begins, "If you haven't buzzed about mauve since the Reagan Administration..." Gosh, I think it's been longer than that. In fact, I can't remember the last time I buzzed about mauve. Wait, maybe it was when ...no, no, that wasn't mauve. Maybe I buzzed about Puce, or possibly Burnt Umber.

Anyway, this celebrity make-up artist (by the way, I don't recall seeing that as a job category on any of those psychological profile exams they used to administer to hapless students. My profile said I was best suited to be a beekeeper. I often look back and wonder, "What if...?")

Where was I? Anyway, the celebrity make-up artist threw in this useful tip: "Dust shoulders, collarbone, cheekbones and ridge of nose with Max Factor Color Genius Bronzer ($8.49) to help unify body and face." Oh, honey, it's gonna take way more than eight bucks to tackle that job. And we haven't even gotten to the unity of body and soul, or heart and soul. Wonder if Max Factor has anything for that?

Well, I could go on, but the boys are back from watching the Speed Channel. Girls, don't knock that station: the one time my husband and I had the same extremely high level of interest in the same TV program was when Jeremy Irons made a guest appearance on "Orange County Choppers." We were both slack-jawed in ecstasy, although for different reasons (I hope). Who says there's nothing good on TV?

Shopping Column
September 3, 2008

Our older daughter and I wanted to help prop up the tottering economy, so last week she and I made the pilgrimage to Oak Brook, clutching fistfuls of gift cards and vowing to shop 'til we dropped.

Not being the real shoppers in the family, we dropped pretty fast; in fact, I'd say we were in free-fall after an hour, but we weren't about to admit it. Female pride, you know: didn't want to let down the team.

The chief problem is that shopping is such an exhausting, unrewarding experience. Plus, the stores we sampled had several alarming characteristics in common. There's the loud rock music at a decibel level designed to discourage rational thought. It's difficult to analyze questions like, "Did I get rid of that blue shirt with the sweat stains, which is the only shirt I own that's long enough to tuck into those preposterous low-riding jeans the kids talked me into getting, or not?" with Nine-Inch Nails pounding in your eardrums.

Then there are the sales clerks who pounce as you walk in, eager to explain the day's many terrific bargains. They mean well, I guess, but they catch me at a bad moment: I'm shopping, see, so by definition it's a bad moment. I wander aimlessly among the racks and stacks of clothes, selecting a few of the less laughable garments. The sales clerk -- strike that -- the sales associate, who has been shadowing me with the finesse of a CIA agent, moves in at once.

"Can I get a room started for you?" she inquires, deftly relieving me of my burden. I nod dumbly, suddenly depressed by the realization that, oh yeah, I have to try the damn things on. She murmurs into her headset as she swishes toward the dressing room. Who is she talking to? What is she saying? It's about me, I'm sure. You're making fun of my fashion choices, aren't you? Well, get in line, sister: dozens of people have done a better job of that than you.

I slink into the little cubicle, with its overly harsh fluorescent lights and overly large mirrors, and begin the degrading task of undressing. Two minutes later, my helpful sales associate is outside the door, asking, "How are those tops working out for you?"

"How do you think they're working out for me?" I snarl (to myself). "Do you see me dancing in the hallway like Mama Mia Meryl Streep?" Instead, I mumble, "Fine," and continue struggling to avoid looking at my reflection: tough with mirrors on three walls.

"Come on out, Mom," my daughter calls. She's in the cell next door, happily trying on business suits even though she has no job yet: hope springs eternal. Reluctantly I emerge, wearing clothes that are clearly wrong in size, style and message. "You look great!" gushes the associate. She's working on commission: what does she care how I look?

"You really think so?" I snarl (again, to myself). "Maybe you'd like it if I waltzed out onto the store floor in this get-up. Your other customers would flee screaming in terror, and then where would you be?"

"I'm not sure it's me," I falter. My daughter opens her cubicle door to look and smiles broadly. Her pin-striped suit is expensive and ill-fitting. "You look great!" says the associate to my daughter. My snarl returns: "Have you no shame? Or are you just on auto-pilot?"

Again I suppress my inner beast: "Honey, why don't we put that on hold, and do a little more shopping elsewhere?" We make our escape, my daughter looking back over her shoulder longingly at the pin-stripes. "Prisoners wear pin-stripes too," I remind her (a little out of date, probably, but neither of us has spent enough time in prisons to know better).

We summon up enough energy to make a few more stops, but our hearts aren't in it, and we limp home with little to show for our efforts: a few garments we didn't really need, a few tubes of body lotion and lipstick. We have to lie down and apply cold compresses to our foreheads.

We'd done our part for economic recovery. Now it was someone else's turn to belly up to the buzz-saw and shop 'til they dropped. Godspeed, fellow shoppers. Don't forget your gift cards. And your Prozac.

Forbidden Fashion
November 5, 2008

  Ever since my kids prohibited me from wearing a jean jacket and jeans at the same time -- they called the ensemble an Arkansas business suit, or a Tennessee tuxedo, or something similarly catty -- I have tried to decipher the hidden code of fashion, but to no avail. So if any of you out there can help me with the following conundrums, please do so:

  -- Just when I finally was able to tuck my shirttails into my pants without the waistband button flying off and blinding an innocent passerby, tucking-in has become a fashion faux pas. Instead, you must now wear your (multiple layers of) shirts outside your trousers, with the hem of the bottom layer showing just a bit (not too much now) below the hem of the next layer. Who decided that? Certainly not a menopausal female, for whom multiple layers of clothing are anathema (that's Greek for, "Don't get me started.").

  -- Flip-flopping is no good for politicians, but mandatory for the young smart set. Remember that photo of the Northwestern women's field hockey team at the White House, with a good 90% of those ladies wearing flip-flops? At the White House? The sound of their parents' forehead-slapping could be heard for miles. And I can personally attest that flip-flops are year-round attire on college campuses in Minnesota. In Minnesota! I guess once the frostbite sets in, you really don't feel the cold. Or anything.

  -- Apparently pantyhose are obsolete, maybe as a result of the flip-flops (which, by the way, we used to call thongs until that term was appropriated by the garment we used to call a G-string, which is also the term for the lowest string on the violin; see J.S. Bach, "Air on the G-String." Have I had too much caffeine?) Anyway, pantyhose are going the way of the dinosaur and the videotape among the youngun's, who waltz around bare-legged. Just you wait, my pretties, until varicose veins take up residence on those gams of yours, and you shop frantically for some good old pantyhose, but they aren't around anymore, because you drove the manufacturers out of business with your negligence, until finally, in desperation, you call your mothers in the nursing homes where you put us, and you ask if you can "borrow" our carefully preserved pantyhose, and guess what? We're going to pretend we don't know what you're talking about.

-- And here's Number 1 on the Makes No Sense To Me list: the I-can't-be-bothered-with-shaving-my-face look. For men, I mean. Well, for women too, I guess, but the problem appears most pronounced among men. Perhaps it is a way of nonverbally identifying themselves as male to the opposite sex, but listen up, pal: if your body, voice and affinity for making Three Stooges noises haven't already tipped me off as to your gender, the chin stubble is not going to be the tie-breaker.

I have also heard that the unshaven look is intended to separate the men from the boys, particularly the ones with baby face looks: you know, "I'm a big boy: I have facial hair." News flash: grownups own razors and know how to use them. Hint: they work better when you install a blade.

Let Mommy or Daddy show you how.

P.S. We all have November 14 circled on our calendars, don't we? That's the opening of the new James Bond movie, "Quantum of Solace" (rhymes with "Wynton Marsalis"). I look forward -- believe me, how I look forward -- to viewing Daniel Craig's well-developed acting techniques, and reporting on them to you. Sigh.

3-2-1 Contacts
February 25, 2009

There are some things you're better off not knowing. I don't mean the obvious stuff, like what your kids are doing while they're away at college, or, for that matter, what your parents were doing while you were away: topics best left untouched.

No, I mean you are better off not knowing what you really look like when you're not wearing glasses.

This thought crosses my mind frequently these days. At the ripe old age of 55, I allowed my silver-tongued optometrist to talk me into trying contact lenses. "It'll take 15 years off," he assured me. "Wouldn't you like to dial it back to 40, Sal?"

I quickly remembered that Daniel Craig is 40. "Sign me up, doc," I chirped.

Never having been able to adjust to bi-focals, I had spent the last several years armed with two sets of glasses (one for distance, one for close-up), subject to jeers and cutting remarks about my goofy appearance. And that was from family and friends. Lord knows what my enemies were saying.

It certainly was a nuisance, carting around all that eyeware -- plus the clip-on sunshades, which really prompted caustic comments from my kids, who have apparently forgotten the years I spent changing their diapers and spooning creamed carrot baby food into their maws. You owe me, ingrates! Fewer demeaning remarks, for starters.

Anyway, here's the point. When you don't see all that well without glasses, you don't know what you really look like without 'em, because as soon as you take off the specs, the world reverts to a pleasing blur, including your reflection in the mirror. It's as if a master photographer had done a bit of air-brushing on your face, only you weren't really conscious of it.

But then you get these soft little pieces of film over your eyeballs, and you take a good close look at your reflection. Aarrgghh! Is that what people have to look at when I'm not wearing glasses?

Woof! The better I see, the worse I look. It's like the first time you heard your own voice on a tape recording. You recoiled in horror, n'est-ce pas? Somehow the recording got everyone else's voice exactly right, then inexplicably screwed up when it came to yours.

I squinted at the mirror in disbelief, feeling like Boris Karloff after Dr. Frankenstein removed the bandages from the bride's eyes. As they say in the optometry biz, didn't see that one coming. Har har.

This did not dial it back to 40. No 40-year-old, unless they've had a very hard life, would look like this. Daniel Craig is going to see through this ploy and continue to ignore me.

Sigh. There's always an unexpected dark side to a good thing, isn't there? For instance, when you quit smoking, as I did years ago, you are assured that food will taste better. Well, that's not exactly true: you will taste food more accurately, which can surprise you. I discovered, once I could really savor it, that I didn't like Szechuan food at all. When I think of the hours I spent wolfing down General Tso's chicken, deluding myself into enjoying it! What I was really enjoying was the tangy combination of nicotine, tar and plum sauce.

So there's the trade-off. If you taste flavors more accurately, you find out what stuff really tastes like. If you see more accurately, you find out what you really look like. That may be information you aren't ready for. As we get older, those pebbles of wisdom become lodged in the shoe of life, providing endless sources of irritation the more we walk down the path of experience.

OK, how about: the chicken bones of wisdom get stuck in the garbage disposer of life, producing a loud grinding noise the more we ignore them.

Or, to paraphrase Bob Seger: wish I couldn't see now, what I couldn't see then.

Flu-Schmoo!
May 20, 2009

  By the time this column sees the light of day, the swine flu ---- Oops! Sorry, Iowa pork producers! My bad! I meant, " the N1H1 flu," as we common folks call it (don't you? I do!) ---- anyway, That Flu may be just a candidate for membership in the "Whatever Happened To . . . ?" club. Let's hope so.
  However, if That Flu has receded in significance, it won't be because of anything the smarty-pants scientists at the World Health Organization or the Centers for Disease Control did. Vaccines? Preventive protocols? Handwashing? Hah! Most of the real sickness experts in the world would scorn such half-baked measures.
  When I was growing up, those experts ---- moms of school-aged kids ---- operated on the assumption that if you were well enough to wake up, you were well enough to go to school. Virtually anything short of a coma-inducing fever or a compound fracture (you know, the kind where the bone is visible, and in fact has popped through the skin to say, "See? She's not faking!") . . . like I say, anything short of those calamities would not buy you a "Get Out Of School Free" card. Those cards are handed out now at the drop of a face mask.
  At best, you might get a visit to the doctor; certainly not a trip to the hospital. Going to the hospital was something you did by appointment, which your doctor arranged for you, like a social secretary; it would be rude to just appear unannounced at a hospital. And a person only went to the hospital to undergo surgery or to die. The doctor's office was for everything else.
  Usually, if your mom let you stay home from school, you probably felt too miserable to really appreciate the day off, which was just how Mom wanted it. First of all, you were confined ---- shall we say, quarantined? ---- in your bedroom. And no TV: this was the time before a TV in every room. The television was a big honkin' piece of furniture that was so powerful it had its own room . . . the TV room, its den, from which it never stirred until the day it

died.

So you were up in your bedroom with, at best, a little transistor radio under your pillow, which you kept on as long as you could hear Mom running the Hoover or Electrolux downstairs. When the roaring of the vacuum stopped, you quickly turned off your radio and whipped it back under the pillow, so that when Mom came in with your aspirin (Tylenol not having been invented yet -- how did we survive?) and your glass of salt water to gargle with, your look of despair was genuine. Most of the time we got better just to avoid the aspirin and salt water.

Lunchtime brought the universal health food: soup. And not any fancy-schmancy soup either (not that there were any, in that era). Progresso and Wolfgang Puck are all well and good when you're all well and good, but for real germ-fighting power, nothing beat the m'm m'm good, watered-down titrate of MSG known as Campbell's soup.

Sometimes we got Chicken Noodle; sometimes we got Scotch Broth, which was always mystifyingly sub-titled "A Hearty Soup" (News flash: nothing under the old red-and-white label could ever have been mistaken for "hearty." That, again, was Mom's point: she was feeding you slightly flavored water, solely for hydration purposes.)

Campbell's appears to have discontinued Scotch Broth, by the way, so if anyone spots it on a grocery shelf, or the back of a tipped-over delivery truck on the Tri-State, send me a silent alarm ASAP. I'll be there in five, ready to barter: I'll trade two of Puck's organic minestrones for one Campbell's Scotch Broth and a player to be blamed later. Just like the Bears!

To be continued . . .

Dang! Once again I have run out of space before running out of stuff to say! And I haven't even gotten into my husband's childhood experiences with sick day procedures, which seem to have involved mustard plasters and ritual incantations and really GOOD soup. So, put this column on the refrigerator next to the Kohl's coupon, and wait for the sequel. Stay well!

Shower Power
July 1, 2009

      You know, when your leg's in a cast, like mine temporarily is, the only thing you can totally immerse yourself in is self-pity. You dream of long, luxurious showers in which you will actually feel as blissful as those folks in the shampoo commercials look, as they lather up in ecstasy.

      Of course, real-life showers aren't like that, even when you're cast-free, are they? In real life, you get shampoo in your eye. You discover that someone (perhaps yourself) has used up the last of the conditioner, and left an empty bottle for you. And you have to turn off the water at least once during every shower to shout to your family, in a voice that can be heard several zip codes away, such pleasantries as, "Who started the dishwasher? Turn that [bleeping] thing off!" or "Answer the [bleeping] phone! Am I the only one who can hear it?" or "Let the [bleeping] dogs out!" (after they have nosed their way into the bathroom in desperation). Me-time, indeed.

      In contrast, in TV Land, the shower model puts her face right up to the showerhead, with closed eyes and a dreamy smile. Clearly she is not in my house, where such a move could result in disaster after a sudden change in water temperature. The only other person you'll ever see look so happy in the shower is Janet Leigh in *Psycho*, right before she gets that surprise visit. That's <u>another</u> reason why I never stick my face up to the showerhead: you never know when someone's going to come at you with a carving knife. What a way to go: lather, rinse, but no repeat.

      What else do they do in shampoo commercials? Let's see: sometimes the model is transported to a tropical waterfall (minus the slippery, moss-covered, jagged rocks, the frogs, the floating leaves and sticks), using a product with a name like Sea Island, which I suppose is a better name for a fragrance than Low Tide, or Dead Carp.

      And have you noticed that on TV, when a man is shown shaving his beard, he is standing in front of a bathroom sink, looking in the mirror, which is pretty much how it goes in real life.

But they're never going to show a real-life woman shaving her leg, are they? Commercials for women's shaving products usually just have the camera zoom in on the woman's calf, covered with a thick, even coating of what appears to be sour cream, as she slowly draws the perfectly clean razor (probably with a clean blade) up her leg, making a beautiful straight furrow through the sour cream.

Where is she? There's nothing in the background to indicate that she's in the bathroom because, hey, there's no background at all, just the sour cream and calf. Where is she? I'll tell you, my friend: she's in a non-existent parallel universe, one in which female shaving is an activity that the bathroom was actually designed to accommodate.

The biggest pain in the calf here is the physical logistics: if we're taking a shower, we prop a foot up on the window sill, or on that tiny corner area of the tub; or we shave during a bath, stewing in our own effluvia, marinating like a chicken breast getting ready for the grill.

And good luck shaving in a motel shower, where they favor smooth, cleanable walls, with no shelves or ledges to start a mildew farm.

The equivalent situation for a guy, I suppose, would be a bathroom with no mirror, so that if he tries to shave, he would have to find some other reflective surface to work with. He could do it, but it would be annoying and inconvenient.

Welcome to our world.

People, if we can put a man on the moon, surely we can put a woman in a shaver-friendly shower.

Or maybe you were waiting for the French to invent one?

The Masked Avenger
July 8, 2009

Last time we were together like this, we were ranting about showers, weren't we? And by "we," I mean all right-thinking folks. For many people, shower time is their me-time; for others, the cocktail hour is their me-time. And then there's this person I read about in an article (in the Wall Street Journal!!) recently, "A Beauty Expert Finds Some 'Me Time.'" The article described how a woman who is a corporate director of beauty services at a fancy spa gives herself a weekly facial at home. (Does her preference for DIY home facials say something about the quality of the facials the spa would probably provide for her, gratis, as the director of beauty services? Or maybe she fears what the employees would do to her face, given half a chance. I'm thinking Mean Boss Lady, but you decide for yourselves.) The quotes below are from the article; I can't make this up.

First, "she tells the family to leave her alone in the bathroom for half an hour" -- and they do! With a family that well-trained, who needs me-time? My family would assume that I was digging a tunnel out of there, like in *The Great Escape*. They'd probably pitch in.

Then, she lights a candle "to create a relaxing ambiance." I'd just wait until one of our famous power outages, courtesy of ComEd, when you can have a relaxing ambiance in the whole house, often for hours on end.

Next, she uses "an exfoliating scrub with jojoba beads to get rid of dead skin." I thought that's why God invented wash cloths, but I'm old school. What is a jojoba bead? I don't know, but it's fun to say, like JarJar Binks in *Star Wars: Phantom Menace*. Then she rinses that stuff off and proceeds to "pore-cleansing extractions," which involve tea-bags in a bowl of hot water, and a towel over her head, as she sticks her face over the bowl for a few minutes and hopes that nobody comes to the door. "Then, she'll examine her pores and do what she can."

Call 911, I imagine. That's what I do after I've examined my pores.

Anyway, her next move is to put on a home-made "skin-care

mask," consisting of avocado, egg, yogurt and coconut oil. Are you thinking "mask" as in Jim Carrey's *Mask*? Me too. Maybe it's the avocado. She "slathers it on" (their verb, not mine), puts on eyepads and a little Enya in the background, and lies down for a 15-minute rest. No wonder: the gal must be exhausted. And exfoliated. In the music department, I might prefer Sinatra's "I've Got You Under My Skin," but maybe she lacks a sense of humor. I suppose the 15 minutes of rest gives the remaining goop a chance to turn into a fine appetizer for later that night.

Time's up! She removes the mask with "a mildly exfoliating sponge" (Again with the exfoliating! How much dead skin can one person have? This is sounding like what they had to do to clean up Leo DiCaprio in *Man in the Iron Mask* after his seventeen years of imprisonment). Next, she puts on some eye cream (not to be confused with ice cream, which would clash with the avocado), "always using her ring finger so you won't pull that skin." That's assuming there's any skin left to pull.

She's almost done. She dots her face and neck with "a pea-sized amount of hydrating moisturizer containing anti-oxidants such as goji berries, to protect your skin from all the free radicals flying around."

What are goji berries? Are they related to jojoba beads? How do you avoid getting smacked in the face by a flying free radical (Bill Ayers, maybe?)? So many questions, so few answers.

People, I don't make the news, I just report it.

The Swimsuit Issue
August 11, 2010

    Working in the garden is a great way to look productive while you're contemplating the world's problems. And if, like me, you have a regular garden-variety garden, you spend a lot of time in it, because you weren't bright enough to buy the plants that thrive on neglect.

    In any event, the other day, I was in the midst of digging up dandelions and planning how to expand the various parts of the Ho-Chunk Casino in the Wisconsin Dells to incorporate some Native American themes: I had decided on the Trail of Tears golf course and the Wounded Knee fitness center and the Broken Arrow archery range, when I was distracted by the arrival of the mail. My train of thought derailed, or at least jumped to a new track, as I thumbed through the summer catalog from Victoria's Secret.

    I'm not Vicky's target audience, by any means. Looking at their swimsuit models, I can see that my demographics are . . . well, let's just leave my demographics out of this. Vicky's certainly did. Actually, Vicky's left a lot out, in terms of fabric anyway, so those supermodels were posing on the beach with a great deal of their demographics showing.

    (How I got on Vicky's mailing list is beyond me; no doubt one of my twenty-something daughters, in a cruel stab at humor, is responsible.)

    Vicky's models do not seem to be up for chopping wood or playing in the snow with Irish setters, the way L.L. Bean and Land's End models are. Vicky's models probably subsist on 60 calories a day, and are too weak and emaciated to do much more than strike a pose. They are probably held up by guy wires during their photo shoots.

    And yet. Here they were, having invaded my home. They troubled me. They mocked me with their pouty lip implants and their wild manes of tousled hair and . . . yes, their two-piece swimsuits.

Guys don't understand, but one of the rites of passage for American women, ushering us into the Middle(Aged) Kingdom, is switching from a two-piece to a one-piece. Our fingernails dig into the doorframes of our youth, as we cling tenaciously to the vision of what we once were. Finally, after the second or third child, we are dragged sobbing into the Misses' section of life. No more flashing that tummy at the world, lady, nobody wants to see it.

Eventually, we resign ourselves to our fate, recognizing that we have taken yet one more step into GrownUpLadyLand. We get a bathing suit that has more fabric than all the rest of the family's suits put together.

But no!, I say, shaking my rolled-up VS catalog in my fist. I will not go gentle into that good maillot! So I went to Kohl's, where they inexplicably sold me a two-piece suit. What kind of irresponsible merchandising was that? How could they allow me out the door with that thing? I know they have cameras in the dressing rooms, so somebody must have seen me put it on. Didn't they have an obligation to me, to say nothing of the world at large, to stop me? And yet, not only did they let me buy it, they gave me 15% off. Talk about rewarding bad behavior. They should have charged me 15% more, stood me in the corner and made me think about what I'd done.

But no. I waltzed out of there with a style of suit I haven't worn since Ronald Reagan was president. Buyer's remorse and wearer's terror set in immediately. I ran to the YMCA to start getting my demographics in shape for public display. While there, I casually mentioned to a few women that I had gotten a two-piece swim suit; they responded with stricken looks, as if my purchase was one of the Seven Signs of Dementia the AARP lists in its helpful pamphlets about aging gracefully.

That night, I modeled my suit for my husband, who loved it, but he's contractually obligated to ("in sickness and in health"), so he doesn't count. My daughters have seen it and given their grudging acceptance, with the caveat that under no circumstances may I be seen by anyone they know or might know in the future.

Fair enough. In the meantime, as I strut along the Lake Michigan shoreline (in Michigan, of course: acceptably far enough away), I flaunt my demographics for all to see. That's right, my eyes say to the passersby, you know you want it. Well, this is your lucky day, pal.

Kohl's is having a sale!

What Lies Beneath
January 27, 2010

How did we women get conned back into wearing girdles again? Call it shapewear or Spanx or whatever: I know a direct descendant of a whalebone corset when I see it. For about a minute and a half sometime in the 1970s, it was permissible to do without all of that, but then the window of freedom slammed shut, and we were once again encased in our Iron Maiden(form) unmentionables.

Actually, the whalebone corset had the advantage of allowing you to go commando, so to speak, whereas our modern contraptions require you either to completely disrobe in order to go to the bathroom, or to try to finesse the garment's patented double gusset crotch opening. We'll just let the curtain of modesty fall on that scenario.

Amazingly, there is not a male fashion counterpart to our corsets. What an oversight! I'm sure men are begging for something they can strap themselves into that will suck in their bellies for them, restrict their breathing and force their paunches up to their armpits or down to their knees. It's only natural.

Instead, men's clothing goes the other way, as with Sansabelt slacks, whose waistline g-r-o-w-s with his budding silhouette. Oh, that's fair.

And women get imprisoned above the waist as well. Remember Jane Russell, who looked great until the day she died, doing commercials for the Playtex 18-Hour Bra? She announced, "Full-figured gals should celebrate!" Well, of course they should. Who ever said they shouldn't? Apparently what Jane meant was that, at last, chesty women were able to wear an undergarment that didn't cut into their shoulders. I'm happy for them.

Meanwhile, in these rapidly changing times, we receive Victoria's Secret catalogs in our homes (without even the dignity of the brown wrapper which hid VS's predecessor in soft porn, the Frederick's of Hollywood catalog, from the mailman's prying eyes). We get to compare ourselves to a creature which exists only in air-brushed fantasy, like a unicorn or a liberal Republican, the busty but extremely skinny girl.

Not a product of nature at all, but wholly man-made, she strides confidently, near weightlessly, through the VS catalog, in jeans which appear painted on, or a business suit with a thigh-high slit. In the lingerie section, her cups runneth over, and her underwear is in the language of dipthongs.

Her facial expressions are alternately pouty and sultry, difficult to describe except to say that they are very different from those in the L.L. Bean catalog. There, the women are hale and hearty pioneer types, usually accompanied by an Irish setter. I shudder to think what the women in the VS catalog would be doing with or to an Irish setter, but I don't think PETA would approve.

The underwear in the LLB catalog is of the long variety, the kind you wear when you're outside chopping wood with an Irish setter nearby, or inside curled up in front of a crackling fire, cradling a cup of hot cocoa, brought to you by the Irish setter, who is sitting in the comfy chair reading the Wall Street Journal.

Meanwhile, back on this planet, the rest of us are spilling Swiss Miss all over the microwave and dealing with our kids and our spouses and a lousy economy. We leaf through the catalogs for escape, and instead are reminded yet again of our . . . shortcomings.

You bet we're bent out of shape.

Section 5: Hearth And Home

This #$%^&*! Old House
August 29, 2007

If our house were a person, it'd be an 85-year-old on life support, and the family would be huddled worriedly in the hospital conference room, trying to decide what to do about Gramps.

Instead of a neurologist, a cardiologist and an oncologist offering their advice, we would have a plumber, a carpenter and a heating contractor, all shaking their heads regretfully.

A building inspector would be leaning against the doorway, vetoing each suggestion with a smirking, "Fraid that wouldn't be up to Code." The Orkin man would pop in periodically to report on termite and carpenter ant infestations. And our accountant would be off in a corner with the mortgage lender, pleading for more money on our behalf, while the lender sighs, "What part of 'No' don't they understand?"

How did Gramps come to be in this sad state of affairs? Throw another log on the fire, and I'll tell you the story. No, wait, the fireplace doesn't work anymore . . .

We bought our dream cottage in 1985 because my husband and I both got a certain vibe from the place. Turns out the vibe was low-level carbon monoxide poisoning caused by a slightly malfunctioning furnace. We'd been house-hunting in August, of course, so who knew from furnaces?

We were captivated by the charm of an older home. Of the three bedrooms, two were microscopic, but what of it? We only had one child at the time, and she was pretty small herself. The point was that the master bedroom was enormous. At least, compared to our 10' by 12' apartment bedroom, it was enormous. Seems kinda cramped now, but maybe that's because the stuff in the bedroom has gotten bigger since then: the bed, the TV, us . . .

The bedrooms weren't long on closet space either. As in, I'm not sure there were any closets in the place when it was built in the roaring 20's. By the time we got there, in the raging 80's, the closets looked like they'd been shoe-horned in by some exasperated predecessors who'd finally tired of hanging their clothes on pegs on the wall.

One and a half baths seemed like a lot, compared to the one bathroom in our apartment. We might have thought differently if some visitor from the future had warned us, "Beware, earthlings. You will have two daughters who will become teenagers, and someday all four of you will need to shower, shave and shampoo within the same 45-minute time period. A rift in the space-time continuum will be your only hope."

None of this mattered because the house had the coolest feature in the world: a third floor attic which had been converted into a bedroom for a sullen teenager (the black wall hangings were the clue). It was a bit warm up there that August (did I mention there was no air conditioning in the house?), so the sweat streaming off our foreheads into our eyes blinded us to the fact that you could fry an egg, melt chocolate and probably liquefy solder on the third floor. We dreamed of having our desks and study area for the kid(s) up there.

Again, Marty McFly was not there to tell us that desks of the future would need computers and printers and fax machines and scanners, each of which would require personalized box fans blowing air on them night and day from May to October, so that the noise on the third floor is comparable to what you hear while standing on the tarmac at O'Hare.

The best feature of the house, of course, was the Motivated Sellers. They were motivated by a pending divorce decree and had long since vacated the premises. We signed on the line, and the rest is history.

To be continued . . .

Sally Sotos is unable to complete this tale of woe within the generous space allotted to her this week. What a blabbermouth. So put this article on the refrigerator and wait for the sequel.

This #$%^&*! Old House: The Sequel
October 10, 2007

As I was saying...

So we buy this old house in 1985. We should have realized the Real Estate Gods were unhappy with us when my husband was hospitalized with viral encephalitis 48 hours before the moving van was to arrive at the apartment. He had to undergo a lumbar puncture and endure an ax-in-the-eye headache and a 105-degree fever; I had to cope with the movers and our one-year-old kid.

I would gladly have traded.

Fast forward twenty-two years, three additions and two refinancings. We've learned a lot. For example, we've learned that the sump pump runs continuously because the house was built over an underground river. We were wondering why the pump was busy during the '88 drought; now we know.

We've learned that building codes no longer permit staircases to be built at the steep angles ours has. And since our front door is positioned directly at the foot of the stairs, you can climb onto a plastic snow saucer on the third floor, have your sister prop the front door open, and wheeeeee your way straight down from the attic right out the door, down the concrete steps and almost all the way to the street. Well, you can do that once.

What else? We've learned that an electrical panel sized for 1920's-era appliances is going to be overtaxed by those from the 1980's. Did you know that electrical fires produce very little smoke and thus will rarely trip your smoke detectors? I know that... now.

We also deduced that our unfinished basement was once a dirt-floor root cellar, because of the alarmingly low ceiling clearance: the current linoleum / concrete combo was probably a few inches above the original flooring. How had we six-footers missed that on our walk-through? Had we even gone down the basement? On the bright side, it means we didn't lose much in the '87 or '07 floods, which actually gave the place a good washing.

Did I mention that we put three additions on the house?

Turns out additions are like tattoos: you think you're going to be satisfied with one, and then you aren't, because you realize how there's plenty of room for another one, and you don't remember how much the previous one hurt going in, because the mind blocks out the memory of pain.

Since our three home improvements were done at different times with different contractors, different architects and, most importantly, different budgets, they bear no relation to each other or to the overall appearance of the house, which now has a startling resemblance to Mad Ludwig's castle in Bavaria. Yeah: being able to match the exterior 1920's brick would have been nice, but no can do, so we opted for dark brown siding instead, which sort of looks like brick if you stand far enough away ... and squint.

But here's the point: remodelling and additions to an older home are like plastic surgery: the patient may look better for awhile, but the aging process marches on.

Which brings us back to the house being on life support. Will propping up that floor or fixing that fireplace really improve our home's quality of life, or simply prolong its agony and postpone the inevitable? Maybe it's time to pull the plug.

Wouldn't it be nice if real life were like TV life, and at the last minute, some super-knowledgeable guy came bursting in with the life-saving diagnosis that would enable us to enjoy many more years with our older home?

Hey, why do you think they call him 'House'?

Sally Sotos and her husband will be putting their home on the curb for the guys in the scavenger truck to pick up.

I Hate Indoor Plumbing!
March 19, 2008

Well, that headline doesn't exactly capture my meaning. How about:

I Fear Indoor Plumbing!

Hmm, that's not quite it either. More like, I Don't Fully Understand How Indoor Plumbing Works (Which Makes Me Feel Stupid, And I Don't Need More Things On THAT List), And Most Of The Catastrophes In Our Home Have Involved Water And Pipes, The Former Not Staying In The Latter.

That's it!

I know, I know. We all have different fears. Some people have a fear of flying, while others fear, for example, bridges. Actually, I have both of those fears. Still others have a fear of clowns. Actually, I've got that one too. Why don't we get back to indoor plumbing...

Let's start our group confessional session by admitting that we don't fully comprehend the mechanics of how a toilet works, and that we are always surprised when the toilet functions during a power outage. There: don't you feel better for owning up?

On the other hand, I used to be surprised that the telephone also functioned during a power outage, until we switched our phone service, and now the phone doesn't work when the power's off. What a relief: it's performing exactly as expected, by not performing.

Back to plumbing. Various kindly people over the years (plumbers, neighbors, guys at the hardware store, husband) have attempted to explain to me the apparently simple mechanism of a flush toilet.

About twelve seconds into the explanation - around when they first use the terms "valve" or "it's real simple" - a fine mist, sometimes an iron curtain, begins its slow descent over my brain, blocking all but the most fundamental operations in there. I am clinically flat-lining.

Well, except my head keeps nodding, and my face keeps looking serious, so my instructor is presumably under the illusion that I am grasping what he's saying. I'm not. Instead, I am thinking, "How can I extricate myself from this tutorial? It's very important that I rearrange my sock drawer right now."

If you're like me in this regard, I'm guessing that your mastery of higher-level plumbing - sump pumps, overhead drains, etc. - is also, shall we say, limited: perhaps enough to fake your way through a cocktail party conversation ("How about those immersible marine battery-powered pumps?" - as universally useful a piece of chatter as, "What the Bears need is a good inside rush," another expression devoid of meaning to me), but certainly not enough, for example, to communicate anything intelligible to the plumber when you make your inevitable frantic call, other than, "There's water all over the basement floor! Come quick!"

When I look down the basement stairs and see the floor glistening, I know it's not because I've been scrubbing the linoleum to a high luster: it's because there's water where there should be no water. And I know that I won't understand why the water is there, even after it's explained to me. Fredo Corleone must have felt my frustration when he cried, "I'm smart, not dumb like they say!"

So here's the point: if we didn't have indoor plumbing, we'd never have water all over the basement floor, and life would be grand. Indoor plumbing may be the greatest thing since bagged lettuce, but I still fear it. Of course, I fear bagged lettuce too, but that's a story for a different day . . .

Sally Sotos does not need you to tell her that she has nothing to fear but fear itself.

Reinvent This!
July 16, 2008

"Reinvent Your Kitchen!"

An attractive notion, I thought, as I paused, on all fours in my unreinvented kitchen, and tried to avoid passing out from the oven cleaner fumes. Whoever named this stuff "Easy-Off" had obviously never used it.

But I digress. "Reinvent Your Kitchen!" was the headline on the slick newspaper insert advertising the annual Kitchen / Bath Industry Show, an insert plastered with pictures of gorgeous, large and, hence, clearly unreal, kitchens. (Sad but true note on life: if they're gorgeous and large, they're not real, guys.) The insert was spread out on the floor in front of the oven, to catch the drips which the cleaning product instructions subtly suggested might damage the floor. Might? Might?? The drip stains on the floor from prior cleanings had peeled the polyurethane faster than paint thinner. More accurate instructions would have counseled the use of HazMat protocols.

Now slightly dizzy from the fumes, I scrutinized the "Reinvent Your Kitchen!" insert more closely. Why is it that pictures of model kitchens so often feature the following?

1. Bowls of fresh fruit sitting on the counter: have these people never heard of fruit flies? Sure, a cute wire basket full of apples looks great, but after you've exhausted yourself angrily swatting the fruit flies in mid-air, you'll remember why one of the big drawers in the fridge is labelled "Fruits and Vegetables." In you go, grannies!

2. Glass-front cupboards with perfectly matched plates and bowls on the shelves: where are the Rubbermaid plastic leftover containers, the World's Greatest Dad mugs, the Brookfield Zoo water bottles? There's a reason my cupboard doors are solid wood: I don't want to have to look at what's in there every time I walk through the kitchen. Let me keep some illusions, please.

3. Open refrigerators stocked invitingly with fresh produce and healthy beverages: get real. Where are the Chinese carry-out containers, the juice bottles with 1/16 of an inch of juice left in the bottom,

the one forlorn Arby's potato pancake? And let's not even ask why the freezers in these ads never contain the blue gel pack (or expired bag of frozen peas) which is constantly in demand for the aches and pains of real people.

4. Perfectly bare refrigerator fronts: no tomato juice splashes, no fingerprints, no magnets, no kids' school schedules or sports schedules or permission slips or report cards, no doctors' appointment cards, no cartoons, no pictures. And we're supposed to believe people live there?

One of the model kitchens in the insert actually seemed to be of normal size and appearance, but it also had three clocks on the wall, labeled "New York," "London" and "Tokyo." Maybe these model kitchen designers constantly need to know what time it is in Tokyo, but I don't. Do you?

Here's a model of a real kitchen:

On your left, you'll see a can of Raid, a permanent fixture on the counter, alongside the aged toaster (shedding bread crumbs like a leper sheds skin flakes) and the microwave (nicknamed Sparky, for dangerously obvious reasons). If you open the microwave door, you'll see the slice of cold pizza, reheated the night before and then forgotten.

The wall nearby contains the smoke detector, whose batteries were removed years earlier because it insisted on springing into action whenever the broiler was used. This kitchen ain't big enough fer both of you varmints, by gum. Next to the disabled smoke detector is the large wall calendar: tomorrow's square says only, "6:00 sharp," with no other explanation. Gulp.

A full laundry basket teeters precariously on the edge of the chopping block. Is the laundry clean (headed upstairs) or dirty (headed downstairs)? Who can tell? It doesn't look too bad: up it goes.

What's that you say? A faint odor of oven cleaner wafts through the room? "Essence of Easy-Off," I call it, as it competes with that subtle but unmistakable room defreshener, Last Night's Popcorn.

Oh, well. I guess reality isn't that great. Maybe I do need to reinvent my kitchen. How about some avocado-and-gold appliances?

Sally Sotos is not sure anyone actually invented her kitchen in the first place, so how can it be reinvented, grasshopper?

Opening the Summer House
July 2, 2008

Ah, yes: visions of sandy feet, towels hung over the back deck railing, lazy golden afternoons spent floating in a giant inner tube. Your trip begins here, in Michigan, just ninety minutes from the Magnificent Mile...

We bolted upright in bed and stared at each other incredulously. The radio commercial for Harbor Country continued, but we couldn't hear it over our stream of shouted expletives. "Ninety minutes? What part of Michigan is he getting to in ninety minutes?" "Maybe he meant Michigan City." "Is he taking the jet pack or the hydrofoil?" "Maybe there's a Magnificent Mile in Hegewisch."

We had set the alarm for 5:00 a.m. that Saturday morning in May, because that was the weekend we had designated for Opening the Summer House, otherwise known as Discovering What Bad Stuff Has Occurred Over The Past Six Months. One year a large branch had been storm-driven through a window; another year the TV set had been stolen. It's never as if anything good has happened up there over the winter, like the neighbors winning the Michigan lottery and deciding, what the heck, let's share with that nice family from Chicago. The best you can hope for is a slower pace of acceleration toward disaster.

Anyway, as anyone with half a brain and only a two-day weekend to work with knows, you set the alarm early because it takes just a wee freaking bit longer than ninety minutes to get up there, and then you turn around the next day and come home, so you want to maximize your time in Harbor Country.

Actually, our place isn't in Harbor Country... more like Harboring Fugitives Country. A bit north of H.C. geographically, but considerably south of it socio-economically. A lot of the natives sound and look like they're from Appalachia, which is OK, just unexpected.

We stumbled across the Township That Time Forgot in the early 1980's, and snapped up a cottage on a bluff overlooking Lake Michigan. That's not all we overlooked. The house was designed and built by its owner-occupant, a strut-wing engineer for Bendix, which may have contributed to my later-acquired fear of flying. The faucets in the kitchen and bathroom were reversed (hot/right, cold/left) and backwards (clockwise, counterclockwise), so that when you tried to turn on the cold water, you were turning off the hot water, which may sound like it would accomplish the same thing, but doesn't, believe me. The hot water heater was the twenty-gallon size. Didn't think they came that small, did you? Twenty gallons does not even get you through a shampoo, and I'm not talking about a "Lather, Rinse, Repeat" version, just one that serves to remove the larger fragments of seaweed and fish bone.

    Did I mention that, like all the other houses in our subdivision at that time, ours was serviced by our own personal septic tank and beach well. (At my husband's insistence, I am now inserting the following language: "And the beach well had a Venturi valve! Can you believe it?!" Happy now, babe?) The house is not winterized, and periodically, despite our best drainage efforts in the fall, the water pipes in the wall develop secret fissures and vomit up their newly pressurized contents to greet us in the spring. Hey, I wonder if this house also contributed to my later-acquired hatred of indoor plumbing.

Will they get the place open before Labor Day? Will the neighbors collect enough signatures to have the Sotos place condemned by referendum? Tune in for the exciting conclusion . . .

Part Two: Michigan Dot Ugh
July 9, 2008

(This is the second part of a column about a summer house in Michigan.)

What else? Our cottage had a rotary-dial phone (still does, actually), which I count as a plus, since our children are now among the few of their generation who can use such a phone without sobbing in frustration. The house's heat was supplied by a cast-iron pot belly stove, which was lovely but also turned out to be the reason we'd have odd headaches and unexpected sleepiness: slow carbon monoxide leaks'll do that to you, I guess.

The view, however, was one thing Mr. Bendix Engineer, the designer-builder-owner of our little nest, couldn't mess up. The west wall is entirely glass, affording spectacular sunset vistas. Of course, the late afternoons of July and August in our one-story, low-ceilinged, un-air-conditioned getaway can be a bit stuffy, as the glass wall serves as a magnifying lens to focus the sun's rays. We adjust the drinking time to start a bit earlier -- OK, way earlier -- on those days.

And because we are in the proverbial Middle of Nowhere, at night you really can see the stars in a dark sky, without that eerie orange haze. The stars are all you can see at night, mind you, so if you want to go for a nighttime stroll down our dirt road, bring a flashlight.

In any event, we finally made it up to our little house in the woods a few weeks ago, and with fear and trepidation, opened the door and made a quick scan. Windows intact; no sign of animal intruders; TV in place. So far, so good. However, as we know, that always means trouble. Sure enough, there was something wrong at several points in the water system, necessitating three trips to the local hardware store.

Not that my husband minds making these trips. This is an old-school, wooden floor, dimly lit hardware store, albeit now Under New Management. The former owner was an older gent who wouldn't sell you stuff he didn't think you needed, so you'd have to explain the nature of your project and methodology to him, and if he didn't think three-quarter-inch pipe was called for, then by God he wouldn't sell it to you. That was true across the board. He wouldn't sell you candy if he thought you were overweight. If a kid came in for a coloring book, the old man would growl, "I sold you one last week. Get outta here." The owner's incredibly aged mother watched TV in a back room of the store, and occasionally shouted instructions to him. He cursed her under his breath while he added up your bill by hand (no cash register, of course).

The new owner is not as gruff as his predecessor, but still pleasingly eccentric. His specialty is knowing everything about every conceivable household project, and spending as much time with you as necessary, so if there is someone ahead of you in line, grab a magazine and settle back, because it'll be awhile.

In any event, he counseled my husband at length regarding our plumbing problems (I overheard, "Now, she's got a tapered thread, so you don't need to worry about overtightening her," which made me wonder briefly what he was really counseling about), and eventually, somewhere around midnight on Saturday night, after a prolonged swearfest, we had running water, i.e., water running within pipes and not all over the thirty-year-old shag carpeting.

Eight hours later, we were back on the road. Halfway home, my husband asked, "Did I cut off the water to the house? That was only a temporary repair: I'm not sure it'll hold until we come back."

I'll let you know.

Sally Sotos is hoping for the best, but could also use the name of a good plumbing contractor who works weekends in Michigan.

It's Alive!
September 24, 2008

I guess it's time to talk about basements again. The recent flooding brought the issue to the surface, so to speak. It's a touchy subject in our house, but writing this column is cheaper than marriage counseling, so here goes.

Saying that our basement is "unfinished" is somewhat misleading; "unstarted" would be more accurate. "Unfinished" also implies some intentional act ("I meant to finish it"), which would be misleading as well.

Finished basements, by contrast, are "finished" in the sense of "done for," "kaput," "terminal." You tempt Fate by finishing a basement because, ultimately, it is still a cellar, an underground den. You can't overcome its basic (lower) nature just by putting good furniture in it. "Finishing" a basement is like putting lipstick on a ... oh, never mind.

Anywho, as far as I can tell, none of the prior owners of our 80-year-old house ever exhibited any interest in, or creative intent toward, the basement at all: it seems to have just appeared spontaneously, its linoleum already chipped and its foundation walls already cracked. Perhaps it was a stray basement, wandering from house to house, forlorn and unloved, until someone took it in, sent it downstairs, and then forgot about it.

Well, it's been down there ever since, like one of those monsters in an old sci-fi movie, lurking behind the mad scientist's laboratory's iron door, waiting for the right moment to strike.

Sometimes the Monster Basement plays it cool, permitting you to hastily enter and exit for laundry and minor food storage purposes. Other times it seems downright benevolent, as it encourages you to store more and more junk (a/k/a potentially useful objects, spare parts, etc.) in its mighty gut. "Someone else's abandoned exercise equipment? Yet another Mixmaster? A powder blue velvet tuxedo jacket, circa 1972? But of course! Be my guest!" it coos.

And so you are lulled into a false sense of security. You take the basement for granted. Meanwhile, it waits. And watches. And waits. And then it strikes.

Perhaps its first move is through the cracks in the foundation. Oh, you'd known those cracks were there, but they didn't cause a problem most of the time, so you'd allowed them to go untreated: festering wounds that added to the basement's anger and self-pity.

Then, a hard rain falls, and the basement seizes its chance to retaliate, granting the storm water full access, tipping over the garment bag holding the velvet tuxedo, destabilizing the shelf of Mixmasters, soaking the brand new 30-pound bag of dog food on the floor.

Now the Monster Basement has tasted blood, and wants more. It decides that some sewer back-up should do the trick, so you watch with horror as the laundry tubs slowly fill, and you realize that connecting the sump pump to the sewer line was just pumping Peter to flood Paul.

Well, you know the rest. The rain stops, and eventually you tame the beast into sulky submission. It has bared its teeth and shown its claws; you should learn your lesson and treat the basement better, but you don't: you get busy, you decide it's too expensive to fix the cracks, etc. Life resumes its old routine.

And the basement watches. And waits ...

Hey, did you just feel a drop?

Now THAT'S A Christmas Present!
December 24, 2008

This year for Christmas, I'm receiving the gift that keeps on giving. No, not an unspayed alley cat; not a Blago campaign contribution. My husband is cleaning out our basement for Christmas!

Understand, when I say, "cleaning out," I'm not just talking abut hauling away broken shelving units and a nonfunctioning fridge. No, no, my friends: as we say in the salad business, that's just the tip of the iceberg lettuce.

We're talking about vacuum tubes and control knobs for radios that haven't been manufactured on this planet since the days of the pharaohs. We're talking wooden tennis rackets. We're talking eight-track tapes (actually, we gave those to my husband's brother, the last person on earth to own a functioning eight-track tape player. Hmm: two brothers who both accumulate ancient useless stuff. It raises the old question: heredity or environment? Either way, I get to blame my in-laws, so it's win-win.).

You learn a lot about a person (not all of it good) when he cleans out your basement. For instance, my husband unearthed a box of our old baby blankets. "I suppose we should give these away," he opined. People, we have two daughters in their 20's; the older one has been going out with the same young man for over five years; and Mr. Clean wants to give away the baby blankets.

"I'm not trying to pour Pedialyte in your punch bowl, hon," I ventured, "but don't you think it's possible that the kids might want these in the near future?" He paused. "What's Pedialyte?" he asked.

I saved the blankets. The spit-up stains are hardly noticeable anymore; plus, they add character. And those blankets (in cheery yellow, because in those days, you didn't know ahead of time which colors to use) were made by doting grandmas, which has to count for something.

One advantage of cleaning the junk out of your basement is that it makes room for good stuff. I know, I know: one person's "junk" is another person's "good stuff," just as one person's hoarding is another person's sensible inventory management, so permit me to disambiguate myself. My definition of "junk" encompasses products that have diminished utility, such as old bandages that have lost their adhesiveness, so that you could bleed to death unless you duct-taped them onto your gaping wound. A lot of those bandages are sitting on the curb now. We kept some for emergencies, of course.

On the other hand, "junk" does not necessarily include products that have simply been discontinued or banned. That red-dye-#2 scare a few years back didn't faze us: we stocked up on some bright red furniture treatment before The Man could tell us not to, and it still works fine. And we're fine. Really fine . . .

Speaking of accumulating discontinued red stuff, we now have room for our fifty large bottles of Scope Cinnamon Ice mouthwash, after the good people at Procter & Gamble, in their misguided marketing wisdom, decided to turn off the spigot on their BEST PRODUCT EVER. Lucky we stocked up early, so we wouldn't have to hoard later.

Our new-found shelf space in the basement also means we can now organize our perishables by die date (a long-held dream of mine), which more or less dictates the upcoming week's menu. No more agonized decision-making over what to serve the fam for dinner; no more consulting them as to what they might actually want for dinner (what a nuisance that was!). Instead, you simply march down the basement, scan the front row of shelf items, and voila! Tonight's special: lima beans! Get 'em while they're still within the implied six-month grace period after expiration!

By now you're probably plenty jealous of my unusual Christmas present. On December 25, you'll be stuck with useless jewelry and Xbox games while I'm reveling in not having to walk sideways between stacks of junk in our basement. I think we know who got the better deal.

Lima beans, anyone?

Green Machines
February 11, 2009

Perhaps this is indicative of a skewed perspective -- like wearing camouflage clothing in order to stand out from the crowd -- but I spend an hour and a half per week watering the houseplants in our home. That's 90 stinking minutes lavished on creatures who show no affection or gratitude for all that attention. I have to talk to them like this:

Yo! Miserable plant life, listen up! This place looks like a hospice! Where has all that water and Miracle-Gro gone? What have you done with it?

All those nutrients wasted. I should have mixed the Miracle-Gro into my salad dressing! The warning label doesn't say it won't work on people, you know: just keep out of reach of children, but, shoot, everything says that. And the list of ingredients sounds a lot like what's in my Flintstones chewables, only a lot cheaper. Miracle-Gro and Wishbone: for the salad lover in you.

In the meantime, you plants are letting me down big-time. You've turned pale and limp, just like me and House. Sometimes, if one of you is particularly sad-looking, I'll put the pot outside in the snow, to serve as an example to the others. Strangely, that seems to make the rest of you even more sullen. What gives?

What am I supposed to do? I can't make the daylight hours last longer. I know it's dry in here, and you don't like that, but I've got three giant humidifiers running on high 24/7, so the place has the decibel level of the tarmac at O'Hare. We have to turn off a humidifier in order to speak without shouting. What else do you want from me?

It's not as if we ask a lot from you. You guys spend your time hanging around, or sitting around, going to pot, veging out, watching "Little Shop of Horrors." You're supposed to be supplying the other part of the oxygen/carbon dioxide respiration cycle, but I can't say I've noticed. If I feel light-headed, I grab an Algerian ivy and hold it to my face for a quick oxygen hit on my way down. What do I get for my trouble? Not oxygen, that's for darn sure.

I've heard that some of you are complaining that you are in macrame hangers. I know they're an outdated holdover from the '70's. Boo hoo. Maybe you'd rather come down and sit on the floor with the rest of your pals, to get stepped on and tripped over. Guess that macrame's looking better, wouldn't you say, bud?

You, tall one in the corner! Don't act like you can't hear me! Word on the street is that you'd like to be dusted more often. Yes, yer majersty! You get dusted just as much as the wooden furniture, and I don't hear them complaining. They remember when they were trees, and life was good. Let that be a lesson.

Hey, don't get me wrong. I know December was a tough month for you. Always is. The new kids on the block come waltzing in: the poinsettias, the Christmas cactus, all decked out in their shiny foil and what-not. You guys get shoved behind chairs to make room for these hothouse floozies. And that's nothing compared to the arrival of Bigfoot the Christmas Tree. Yowza! He gets ornaments and garlands and a star and God knows what else ... and he's dead!

What can I say? Deal with it. Sing "The Holly and the Ivy" to yourselves. Maybe it'll help. In the meantime, here's the bottom line, peeps. I want to see a whole lot more green out of you, really fast. There's plenty more where you came from, believe me. I brought you into this house, and I can take you out.

Or are you interested in volunteering for some stem cell research?

Walls of Ivy
April 28, 2010

We all have hot button issues: topics the mere mention of which will turn us from our mild-mannered selves into Incredible Hulks seething with fury.

My husband's hot button is ivy.

His hatred for ivy began, I suppose, one warm summer night a few years ago. I was lying in bed, minding my own business, when I heard a scratching noise on the window screen behind me. Since our bedroom is on the second floor, I didn't fear an intruder (Now, of course, having since watched several reruns of "Criminal Minds," I would assume such a noise heralded the imminent arrival of a chain saw massacre serial killer. But back then, who knew?).

Anyway, I swiveled my head 180 degrees around (a little trick they teach you when you're in the maternity ward for the first time), when what to my wondering eyes should appear but . . . a little furry face pressed against the window screen, with two beady eyes staring back at me.

My shrieks pierced the quiet summer night, bringing my husband into the room on the run from wherever he'd been savoring a few minutes watching Pinks All Out on the Speed channel. He saw Mr. Furry Face (we deduced later that it was probably a possum), and his eyes narrowed with steely determination (or maybe he was squinting to see across the room without his glasses).

"Wait here," he ordered, and left the room, returning a moment later with a broom --my best broom! -- and whispered, "Open the screen."

"I beg your pardon?" I squeaked in a Henry Aldrich voice. "It almost sounded like you told me to open the screen."

"I did," he replied, gripping the broom as if it were a baseball bat. "He'll run in here, and I'll beat the [noun] out of him."

Does this sound like a plan to you? If you're a guy, it's a great plan, like equipping your car with a jet engine. If you're not a guy, your reaction might be like mine:

"Are you nuts? You're going to bash a possum to death on our bed, so we'll have blood and guts and possum gunk all over the sheets? With a broom? With no glasses? What is wrong with you?"

"It's payback time," growled my husband, still clenching the broom. "This time, it's personal." Guys talk like that in moments of stress, don't they? "Say yer prayers." "Reach for the sky." "Do you feel lucky?"

I racked my brain to figure out what exactly was so personal, finally realizing that he was referencing some prior run-ins we'd had with possums taking up residence under our back deck. This time, though, there would be no animal trapper, no catch-and-release; more like catch-your-lunch.

Fortunately, my sweetie didn't end up bludgeoning the possum that night, the beast having fled back to his nightly lair (probably under the deck) during our argument. Instead, at the dawn's early light, Mr. Broom went outside to investigate how this waddling marsupial made it up to the second floor window. It was then that he found his nemesis, his white whale, his purpose in life.

The possum had climbed the ivy.

For those of you not lucky enough to live in an ivy-covered cottage, let me enlighten you. Remorseless, implacable, unstoppable: ivy develops thick, tree-like roots and runners and branches, as my husband discovered when he began ripping our beautiful ivy down. Of course the possum had climbed up the ivy; I could have climbed up the ivy, it was that strong.

My husband escalated his response to the challenge of the ivy. Where the ivy consisted of small tendrils, he used hedge clippers. Where the ivy got stronger, Paul Bunyan whaled on it with an ax. Where the ivy put one of ours in the hospital, he put one of theirs in the morgue. Wait, never mind: that's just more guy-under-stress talk. It kind of grows on you after awhile.

Like ivy.

Eventually he got rid of all of our lovely ivy, adopting a scorched-earth policy akin to Sherman's march to Atlanta. But eternal vigilance is the price of freedom from ivy, and recently he discovered a few brave vines daring to venture up our brick walls. Out came the ax and the shovel, disturbingly reminiscent of those

"Criminal Minds" reruns. He began excavating at the base of the house, searching for the taproot, when I timidly suggested that perhaps it was the ivy that was actually holding up our otherwise-crumbling foundation. "Whose side are you on?" he snapped.

Boy, you think you know somebody...

As usual, it's the WorldWideInterweb that has come to my husband's rescue. He's discovered killtheivy.com, complete with chat room contributions from IvyKillerIke and IvyLeagueLouie. "I'm not alone," he whispers, his face bathed in the eerie glow of the computer screen. "Did you know that scientists think ivy can grow on the surface of Venus, where the temperature is 900 degrees and the atmosphere is deadly carbon dioxide with frequent acid rains, and the pressure at the surface is like standing a mile deep in the ocean? Ivy can live there!"

I wouldn't be a bit surprised. Go ahead, hon, make my day.

Topical Storm
August 4, 2010

  Still trying to dry out our basement after Mother Nature's latest practical joke. OK, I get it now. I'm a slow learner, but I finally get it:

  1. Do Not Put Valuable Things In The Lowest Level Of Your House. At least until you have a check valve, a really good one, installed in your sewer line. Accept no substitutes. A Czech valve is not the same thing.

  2. But If You Must, At Least Keep The Valuables Off The Floor. This is why God invented pallets. A palette is not the same thing.

  3. Hundred-Year Storms Can Happen More Than Once Every Hundred Years. So, if you thought that the summer 1987 hundred-year storm was buying you a Get Out Of Basement Free card, think again. Ditto re the September 2008 hundred-year storm, and every one since. The HYS, as we in the storm biz call it, is a creature of the law of averages, which as we know is not a law at all, but a figure of speech of absolutely no use in the short run, "short" being defined as "less than millennial."

  4. No Municipality Can Have Sewer Pipes Sized To Handle HYSs. Not in this economy anyway.

  5. Stress Tests Can Come In Many Forms. Sure, you could waste your time on the hospital treadmill, getting rigged up to some fancy machine, and then huffing and puffing in a sterile atmosphere of peace and serenity, with medical personnel standing by. Or . . . you could scramble around in sewer water trying to heave a washer and dryer up onto pallets (see Rule 2) before more bad stuff happens. Your choice. Compare the deductibles first.

  6. Ask Job. You remember Job, to whom Yahweh administered some very special stress tests. Re-read that old story (if your Old Testament has dried out).

  7. We Own A Lot More Stuff Than We Need To. If you forgot you owned something until it floated by you on a wave of

sewage, would you really have ever missed having it at all?

8. Storms Are Mother Nature's Way Of Helping You Downsize. My husband's been "cleaning out" the basement for years, but progress has been slow, sometimes indiscernible. Now: whoa! Nice work, honey!

9. We Don't Really Need To See Our Curbs. They were covered with fallen tree branches, limbs and miscellaneous windfall which we dutifully dragged there from that tornado-like breeze that wafted through here a few weeks ago. Now our curbs are covered with carpet remnants and soaked furniture and junk. Curb your enthusiasm? No problem.

10. Do Not Make Fun Of Tom Skilling's Inaccurate Forecasts Of Heavy Weather. Every once in a while, he's right. Who knew?

11. Things Aren't Important; People Are. Well, unless the things are pictures of people; then, yeah, they're valuable. See Rule 1.

Well, any other lessons learned? Let me know. Elmhurstss@aol.com. Oh, one more:

12. Beagles Are Of Very Little Use When You're Flooded.

Section 6: La Famiglia!

Used Car Shopping, or Who Do You Trust?
July 11, 2007

There are a lot of ways you can lose your innocence. Our younger daughter lost hers while car-shopping.

Our participation in that great American coming-of-age ritual, Buying a Car for the Kid Who Didn't Get Grandma's Car, began calmly enough. First, we had to break the news to Daughter #2 that she was not going to be getting a new car, but rather a used car. She took it rather well, especially after our crisp explanation of the alternative, which involved two wheels rather than four.

(At this point you may be asking yourself, why would you guys buy your kid a car at all, you morons? Ah: I see that you yourself do not have children attending college 400 miles from home, in Minnesota, in particular, a college which makes sure that the fall move-in/spring move-out dates always land on the Labor Day/Memorial Day weekends. A year or two of those treks (which involve passing through The Dells on those weekends - think about that), and the brilliance of getting your kid a car and having her do the drive herself becomes blazingly obvious. The business about the two wheels rather than four was thus the emptiest of threats: she was getting a car whether she wanted one or not.)

Daughter #2 and her father began making the rounds of the 700 car dealers in the area, and she soon fell in love with the car of her dreams, the one that the oily salesman assured her was "a steal of a deal." However, she took the precaution of doing a background check on it via one of those web sites that ought to be named, "Welcome to the Real World, Sucka."

The website report/rap sheet contained an alert in large red capital letters, never a good sign. We learned that the car in question had spent its first year of life as a rental, and that subsequently there arose some issue about the accuracy of the odometer numbers.

My husband shook his head regretfully as he finished reading the report, then noticed that our daughter's eyes were brimming with tears.

"The car's never had a real home," she sobbed. "It's like a little orphan who's been treated badly. It needs tender loving care, and a chance to prove itself worthy."

"Are you nuts?" her father inquired courteously. She sobbed harder.

Fortunately, her older sister - the lucky gal who had gotten Grandma's 1988 maroon Buick LeSabre, the wheels of choice of grandparents everywhere - stepped in. Her Bossy Older Sister tone immediately caused Daughter #2 to stop whimpering.

"Mom and Dad are right," said Bossy Older Sister. "The car is lame. Get over it." And that was that.

The next car that caught Daughter #2's fancy seemed more promising, so she and her father took it out for a test drive, reassured by this salesman's grave vow that since he, too, had a daughter in college, he understood the importance of the car being Absolutely Safe, and he personally vouched for the car's pedigree: "I wouldn't sell anything that wasn't safe."

Two minutes into the test drive, my husband and daughter noticed fine grains - shall we say shards? - of something being blown into their faces via the air conditioning system. It was glass, the remnants of the original windshield, we discovered later.

I am not making this up. Any of it.

Our local mechanics - who had no dog in this fight - did a quick once-over of the car, and opined that it had been through several near-death experiences. They were eager to show us the evidence, and had several yuks at the salesman's audacity. OK, they didn't use the word "audacity."

Daughter #2 was horrified. An adult had looked her straight in the eye and lied about something important. Her father sighed. "How can I put this, sweetie? There is evil in the world. Let's go get a pizza."

Needless to say, she eventually ended up with a car she likes (purchased from an Elmhurst dealer, of course), sadder but wiser.

87 La Famiglia!

Wait 'til she starts house-hunting...

Sally Sotos and her husband drive cars manufactured when Bill Clinton was president.

Tattoo You
December 26, 2007

So our 21-year-old daughter got some tattoos recently. I wasn't surprised: she inherited the tattoo gene from her father, whose upper arms are festooned with colorful images of ... well, throw another log on the fire, and I'll tell you.

For as long as I've known him - since the dinosaurs ruled the earth - my husband has wanted a tattoo. Apparently this desire arose in his early youth, in the mid-1950's, when an older cousin defied the family tribal council and got inked: on one arm was a saber tooth tiger with blood dripping from its fangs, and on the other was a pair of dice with the word "Lucky" embossed in flowing script below.

How cool is that? No wonder my husband worshipped this guy, who also sported a D.A. haircut and an upturned collar on his black leather jacket: the Fonz of Phillips Street in Chicago. Finding high school too confining, Cousin Connie (short for Constantine) married at 16 and added to his legend.

I hasten to add that Cousin Connie is now a great-grandfather, still married to the same woman, gainfully employed, a pillar of his community - and he still has a D.A. And his tattoos. I doubt that his kids / grandkids / great-grandkids appreciate his essential coolness.

Anyway, my husband's life arc diverged slightly from Connie's, but he still yearned for tattoos. I exercised a spousal veto for years; then, worn down, I passed the veto baton to our daughters, confident that they would uphold the proud tradition of women everywhere: nixing guys' urges for ... well, for just about everything.

My crafty husband bided his time, waiting until the older, really uptight kid left for college. Then he struck a deal with the younger, goofier one: she could get her navel pierced if he could get a tatt.

Done and done. He came home with a barbershop pole inscribed on his left bicep and a smile on his face. She came home with a band-aid on her midsection that screamed, "Infection within 4 days, tops," having been pierced by a guy who looked like his day job was running Pharoah's Fury at Elmfest.

Sure enough, the navel ring never worked out, and after multiple attempts, she threw in the (pus-filled) towel and settled for an ear cartilage piercing. By that time, though, such ear work had gone mainstream and thus did not signal the defiance of authority and the assertion of individuality that it had previously, before soccer moms and crossing guards had their cartilage pierced.

In the meantime, my husband (who had SWORN that ONE tattoo was all he would ever, EVER want) decided that he needed another one. I was busy coping with menopause at the time - you don't realize how many windows you have in your house until you have to run around opening them all - and didn't have enough energy to draw another line in the sand.

Grumpy and Goofy were both away at college by now, and the only other family member at home, the dog, was an undependable ally, switching allegiances depending on who offered him the largest quantity of Snausages.

So, the right bicep came home one day with a picture of a World War I recruiting poster on it. Whatever. It was cheaper than buying a Harley or paying for skydiving lessons.

But then the Cartilage Kid got restless, and asked permission (wasn't that sweet?) to have some meaningful excerpts from "The Little Prince" inscribed around her wrists. In French. Whatever. They look like bracelets if you squint.

Don't think I'm a pushover, though: the last time she was home, I made her put on a belt so that her jeans would stop their downward slide toward her ankles and would instead stay somewhere betweeen her equator and her tropic of capricorn.

I run a tight ship, my friends.

E.T., Phone Home!
January 23, 2008

Apparently, there are two kinds of people in the world: (1) those who understand the importance of checking in with loved ones periodically, to assure them that you are alive, and (2) stubborn self-centered beasts who cruelly enjoy inflicting emotional pain on said loved ones.

Take my husband. In the early years of our marriage, before I broke his spirit, he was known to spend an occasional evening with his barbershop-singing buddies, or with a posse of fellow lawyers, or with other ne'er-do-wells from the dregs of society. He would make the mistake of giving me a wildly optimistic ETA: "No later than midnight: it's a weeknight, honey, so 12:30 at the latest."

Tick-tock, tick-tock. So 3:00 a.m. finds me huddled on the kitchen floor, sobbing, having telephoned every police department between home and whatever dive he had alleged he would be patronizing, to see if any accidents or arrests had occurred involving him.

Was I being unreasonable? Stop, don't answer yet. Sure, that was the era before cell phones, but it was still the era of pay phones. Maybe you younger readers have seen them in old movies. They were everywhere, like ATMs and Starbuckses. For a few coins, you could call anywhere, anytime (24/7!) and let someone know that you were safe and not lying in a ditch by the side of some lonely road, next to your overturned vehicle whose tires were spinning slowly to a stop . . .

Anyway, where was I? Finally, of course, my husband does come home, and I'm sure the sight of his wife on the floor, tears streaming down her face, her expression a mixture of relief that she was not yet a widow, and anger that he had screwed up so badly . . . well, who wouldn't be glad to come home to that? Beats me.

Eventually, he figures out how to placate me, and life proceeds smoothly until our oldest offspring hits high school and curfew becomes an issue. We carefully explain to her that the Illinois legislature in its wisdom has decreed what time she is to be home, and what's good enough for the boys in Springfield is good enough for us.

It is only then that we discover that, although she is a smart cookie, she has inherited the Nobody Tells Me What To Do gene from her father, so that once again I am huddled on the kitchen floor, sobbing, wondering whether my Smart Cookie is lying in a ditch by the side of the road.

Does any of this sound familiar?

Finally, after being grounded a few times, and after the advent of cell phones, she gets the message, and our family life again proceeds smoothly, particularly because her younger sister, having observed all of these goings-on, figures out the secret of life:

If Mama ain't happy, ain't nobody happy.

So Daughter #2 checked in constantly throughout high school: "Sshh, you guys, shut up, I'm calling my mom. Hi, Mom, just checking in, everything's fine, I'll be home in an hour."

Now, how hard was that? And she just bought herself an hour's grace period. Duh.

The summer of '07 was a special test of our check-in relationship. Both kids lived and worked in the greater Minneapolis area, and on the night of the bridge collapse up there, right on cue, D-2 assures us promptly that she's OK. We don't hear from Smart Cookie until the middle of the next morning, after the kitchen floor and I have renewed our acquaintance.

Is it me?

Most recently, Smart Cookie did it again in September, when she flew off to spend a year in Belgium. Trying to sound casual, I suggested, before she left, that since she would have a FOUR-HOUR layover at JFK, maybe she could find the time to call home. "I'll try," she smirked. I guess four hours in an airport must really fly by, so to speak, because she just didn't get a chance to check in. She did send us an e-mail from Brussels. I suppose that's progress...

Sally Sotos' younger daughter is spending January in Fiji, and checks in regularly with weather updates.

Mother's and Father's Daze
May 6, 2009

What is the difference between Mother's Day and Father's Day? No smart remarks, please. The correct answer is: Mother's Day harnesses the free-floating guilt that dads feel about moms' lot in life, and channels it in a fashion that is commercially advantageous for restaurants, florists, jewelers, chocolatiers, etc. This has the added benefit of relieving Dad of the burden of discovering what Mom actually wants for Mother's Day.

In contrast, moms have very little free-floating guilt about dads' lot in life, so there is nothing for commercial America to harness for Father's Day. And moms already know what dads want: some nice uninterrupted time in front of the TV, or in the tool aisle of Menard's. Moms know this from observing how dads actually spend their non-Father's Day weekends, because, frankly, every day is Father's Day. Capice?

The irony, of course, is that not all moms are gung-ho for the restaurant brunch thing on Mother's Day, as it busts up the day and requires time to be spent getting the kids hosed down and restaurant-ready. Guess whose job that is?

And let's not even talk about the complications engendered by the presence of one or more grandmas in a hundred-mile radius. Notwithstanding the existence of Grandparents' Day, grandmas generally expect a little recognition on Mother's Day as well. (As usual, the AARP is double-dipping.) And thus another holiday battle ensues, as the grandmas of America, like aged but skilled ninjas, employ the well-honed Nunchucks of Guilt: "You mean you won't have time to come over on Mother's Day? Oh . . . and the house is so empty these days." Tough to think of a snappy comeback to that one, so off you go, over the river and through the woods, to listen to another afternoon of the Angina Monologues.

When our kids were fairly young, they asked me innocently one year what I would like for Mother's Day. Fixing them with a steely gaze, I replied that I would like to spend all day planting flowers in the yard. By myself. Their father hastily explained to them that Mommy loved them very much but needed to really, really concentrate on her pretty flowers.

(If I were a young mother now, I would choose to closet myself in a room with a bottle of wine and a DVD of *Casino Royale*, while my husband explained to the kids that Mommy loves them very much but needs to really, really concentrate on the pretty blond man and his very important card game.)

In any event, our arrangement was win-win! The kids were relieved not to have to get cleaned up; ditto with Dad; the money we would have spent on brunch was devoted to flats of impatiens; and, most importantly, the time I would otherwise have spent laying out their little outfits on their beds, supervising their baths, refereeing their disputes ("I was Skipper last time! I get to be Barbie this time!") and, oh yes, getting myself ready -- all was dedicated to doing something I really wanted to do.

Why shouldn't Mother's Day be a day off from being a mom? Less togetherness, if you please, and more good old quality time for the rest of the family.

Maybe you've already made plans for Mother's Day 2009, but there's still hope for Father's Day. To establish equality between the parental holidays, what if, instead of letting Dad do whatever he wants, we were bombarded with commercial messages telling us that Dad really wants to spend some time in the middle of a Sunday at Egg Harbor with the fam, feasting on some variation of fried scrambled eggs and granola-in-a-glass? Why isn't the American Restaurant Association all over this one? "Make your brunch reservations for Father's Day!"

And we can continue to play turn-about on Father's Day by letting Dad get the kids ready for Egg Harbor, while Mom sits on the edge of the bed in her underwear, slack-jawed, oblivious to the chaos in the bathtub, watching George Clooney and Brad Pitt in *Ocean's 11*.

One special day a year, is that asking too much?

Sally Sotos wishes you all a Happy Mother's Day, and is sorry her own mom is no longer around to spend Mother's Day with.

Crazy Parents!
August 27, 2008

To celebrate the price of gas dropping below $4 a gallon, we decided to take a road trip to Minneapolis recently to watch one of our college-senior daughter's plays being put on at a fringe festival.

Now, that paragraph contains much important information for parents of young offspring. First, your days of journeying long distances to bear witness to your child's prowess in a) sports, b) the arts, c) you name it, do NOT end when the kid graduates from high school; oh no, my friend, your traveling days have just begun. Second, for drama parents, college will offer your child a greater array of options for being unemployed in four years: not just being an out-of-work actor, but also being an out-of-work playwright. Hooray!

Every road trip, of course, has the obligatory leg involving not stopping for directions, not using maps, angry silences in the car, etc. I leave it to you to pick which donkey gets THAT tail pinned on. But that's not my point here, just a detour into Cliche-land.

Speaking of stereotypes, let's talk theater people. Can you spell "flamboyant"? It's a word of French origin meaning, "desperately needing to be set on fire." And a weekend of original (hence the "fringe" in "fringe festival") one-act plays, being put on in rapid succession in a single building with multiple stage areas, brings all the flamboyant, scarf-wearing (in August!), body-pierced, unusual hair-colored, non-soft-spoken folks together *en masse* (that's French for "say your prayers").

Like a densely-packed neutron star, a teaspoonful of which weighs more than the Earth itself, cramming multitudes of drama folk into a confined space results in a huge accumulation of energy, angst and Axe body spray. You know when critical mass has been achieved in this crowd when they break out in spontaneous group renditions of the entire songbook of "Rent." They wear T-shirts with the logos of productions they've been in, with cryptic insider references like "Must Avoid" or "Smell the Heliotrope." They sport odd-looking eyewear, and are incapable of greeting each other without shrieking.

All you can do is repeat, over and over, "We support the arts," through gritted teeth. Sometimes what you really mean is, "We support our kid, and she happens to be in the arts. If she were dabbling in, say, the biathlon, we'd support target shooting and cross country skiing. Whatever."

Supporting a kid in the arts has meant a lot of gritted teeth, hasn't it? In fact, supporting a kid in anything can wear down your molars. For sports parents, it also includes a lot of time: (1) sitting on bleachers designed for spinal columns a lot younger than yours; (2) standing on sidelines in ponchos in the rain; (3) planning holiday weekends around tournaments; and (4) vowing you're not going to be like some of those really crazy sports parents, only to discover, oops, that train left the station a long time ago, and you're on it; in fact, you're the conductor.

The irony, of course, will be that our children will react negatively to all of this parental effort, deciding instead to give their own kids a big dose of Tough Love, causing us once again to grit our teeth as we mutter, "We support our children in their child-rearing decisions." I see a big future in dental implants . . .

Can This Marriage ...
September 10, 2008

The Ladies' Home Journal used to have a regular feature called, "Can This Marriage Be Saved?" As I recall, it would describe the many points of conflict between an actual husband and wife, and then a marriage counselor or two would chime in with advice. Remember?

For example, the wife would be a health food nut, while the husband would prepare himself some chocolate-covered bacon for breakfast. The wife would enjoy watching Cary Grant movies, but the husband would prefer the Three Stooges. You get the idea.

Anyway, I was reminded of "CTMBS?" the other day when my husband arrived home after work with several pieces of used furniture he'd run across and apparently couldn't bear to live without, including an adjustable desk chair in a very surprising shade of purple; a small desk to supplement the eleven (I counted 'em) small desks that have already taken up residence in our home; a cabinet for stereo equipment ("including a shelf for a turntable, honey!"); and a gun cabinet although we own no guns (a condition I am now considering changing).

He proudly arrayed these items in the garage for my inspection. It reminded me of the years when I was a kid, and our cat would kill chipmunks and then line up the little carcasses outside the back door. No matter how many times we screamed, "Eeeewww!", the cat didn't get it. Neither does my husband. I screamed a few words more colorful than "Eeeewww," and repeated my newest threat -- the one replacing the prior empty threats -- to run away. He was crestfallen.

It's like being married to Arthur Weasley, fascinated by objects from the Muggle world.

How had I missed this salient trait when we were dating over a quarter of a century ago? Was I so blinded by the Reagan presidency that I failed to notice how much stuff my new boyfriend had in his cool apartment? (Actually, what had really impressed me was the bowls of M&Ms carefully situated on the side tables in his living room and bedroom. How cool was that? Little did I suspect that, years later, all of our pillowcases would be stained with chocolate drool, the inevitable outcome of falling asleep with M&Ms in your mouth.)

Sigh. You old married dinosaurs know how it is. Turns out Mr. Right thinks his turn to "look after the kids" means just being in the same Zip code with them. Turns out Ms. Perfect doesn't like kung fu movies nearly as much as she led you to believe, so that now when you suggest "Flying Helmet of Death" again for your Saturday night date movie, she's not pleased.

And then the aging process itself adds its own magic. One of you says, "Want anything from the store?", and the other one hears, "One knee thing for his door?" Your kids cut out ads for hearing aids from the newspaper and scatter them around the house. One of you has bum kneecaps, the other has nagging shoulder problems. When did we turn into Mr. and Mrs. Wobble, leaning on each other for ambulatory as well as moral support?

The list goes on. One likes the house cold, the other likes it warm. One likes big dinners, the other wants light suppers. In our house, my husband enjoys reading about the Great Depression, and drawing morbid comparisons to today's economy; I read, "Think Yourself Thin!" and make notes in the margin. He listens to barbershop quartet music; I prefer tenth century plainchant.

So . . . can this marriage be saved? It doesn't matter: I can't run away from home (I can't run anywhere, actually), and now, with that chip in my neck, they'll just return me anyway . . .

Up and At 'Em!
November 19, 2008

The TV commercial that caught my eye the other night portrayed a coughing child in bed, hacking up a storm. I waited for one of the kid's family members in a nearby bedroom to shout, "Shut up in there!" or "No coughing!", which is how we handle coughers in our house.

Instead, the TV kid's mom rushed to his bedside with a bottle of cough medicine and a spoon, apparently intent on medicating him. "What good is that gonna do?" I asked no one in particular. "Now she's gonna get sick too! She should be conserving her strength. The kid'll survive without the cough syrup. Probably."

Then I noticed the really unusual thing: the TV kid was actually under the bed covers! Between his sheets! I couldn't believe my eyes. My kids hadn't slept on their sheets since the day, long ago, that I assigned them the daily chore of making their beds. Being geniuses, and bone-lazy to boot, they had immediately deduced that sleeping on top of their covers, beneath piles of raggedy old baby blankets, meant that the sheets would never get mussed and thus the beds would never need to be made.

That is why the beds of our children, who are now well into their 20's, still have Where's Waldo? and Disney Princesses sheets on them. The sheets are in mint condition, of course.

Pondering the bedclothes business caused me in turn to reflect on the methods parents use to awaken their offspring. My husband's father would leave the house at 5:30 on Saturday mornings, to get to the family meat market; on his way out, he would rap loudly on his kids' bedroom door, shout "Get up!" in Greek, and then depart, leaving the kids to wonder why they needed to get up. If they dared to ask, however, they were met with a response which translates roughly as a promise to remove their viscera. After that, you don't ask again.

I, on the other hand, was awakened, as a child, by my mother's jovial "Get up, get up, you lazy sloth, we need your sheet for a tablecloth!" Where do they get this stuff? This was the same woman whose universal phrase of encouragement was, "Hop to it and get a red nose." What does that mean? We never knew.

Then it came time for my husband and me to awaken our own children. Our older kid turned out to be the kind who snarled and snapped at conventional attempts to get her up. We referred to her as "The Beast," and tried poking at her with a long stick, which only elicited a low-throated "unnnhhh" from her. My husband eventually found that he needed to allot half an hour to the Beast Awakening Process, which required skills akin to those of the Horse Whisperer.

Our younger kid presented a slightly different problem: she sleepwalked, so that you were liable to wake up at odd hours to find a child standing next to your bed, staring unseeingly and speaking like the Rock People from an old Flash Gordon serial: "Grod danodnock vodnu." You'd have to pick her up and carry her back to her bed, which became more cumbersome when she was in her teens.

Awakening a spouse, of course, raises a host of different issues, the primary one being that you're generally trying to stop some offensive behavior, like snoring, which the (allegedly) sleeping spouse is (or pretends to be) completely unaware of. For instance, maybe you've got someone like my husband in your house. (Heck, you may even have my husband himself; sometimes we forget to watch him and he wanders off.)

In my judgment, awakening a snorer is akin to removing a band-aid: it's more merciful to do it quickly and abruptly rather than prolonging the experience. A couple of quick elbow slams into the ribs generally gets the job done. If the condition persists, try shouting "Fire!" while throwing some more elbow jabs. Believe me, they don't snore after that; they don't even sleep.

Thus, your spouse is awake when the sleepwalker comes in, and can take care of tucking her back under her pile of rags. After that, it's just a few more hours until it's time to wake up The Beast. In the meantime, your spouse can watch late-night TV infomercials, and learn how normal people are supposed to raise their kids ...

Silence is Golden
March 4, 2009

As we were lining the birdcages with newspaper recently, we happened to read that Sen. Burris has announced that he will no longer entertain questions from the press about his senatorial appointment.

Good for him! I say, the less talking, the better. For years, I have tried to enforce a "Written Communications Only" rule in our family, although with little success, I must add. Mostly that rule just resulted in other family members exchanging sidelong glances, to the effect of, "Who honked off Mom this time?"

In truth, I invoke the "No Talking" rule when faced with a question or remark to which I have no response. "Mommy, where do babies come from?" "OK, no talking." "Hey, who ate the last piece of pizza?" "Silence begins now." "How come there's no toilet paper in here?" "I said no talking."

Fellow parents who knew me in a previous life, when our daughters played soccer together, will be stunned to learn now of my code of silence: when I was on the sidelines, they could never shut me up. I wasn't one of those moms who'd chatter on, oblivious to the game. Oh no: I was intensely, upsettingly, disturbingly into the game, shouting epithets at the ref and the opposing players. You're thinking about me, "Sal, they were somebody's daughters too." You know what I'm thinking about you? "OK, no talking."

My husband refused to stand near me at games, instead prowling the sidelines pretending to study the pattern of ball control. Frequently, assistant coach Bill would sidle up to him, as if my husband were Fredo watching his wife embarrass herself on the dance floor; Bill would whisper apologetically, "Coach Mike says, if you can't take care of this, I have to." My husband would shrug and say, "I think you'd better." Bill would then wearily plaster a large strip of duct tape over my mouth: OK, no talking, Sal.

At other times, my husband would simply deny knowing me, usually three times, and usually when the ref grew tired of my antics.

"Is that your wife, sir?" "No." "Didn't I see you two come here in the same car?" "No." "Are you sure that's not your wife?" "I don't know her!" I've got your back too, honey. What can I say? I had issues.

You can probably find me on one of those "Unsportsmanlike Conduct!" videos they force parents of sports kids to watch now. There, that's me, my face contorted in rage, shaking my fist, being physically restrained by fellow parents from charging onto the field. Good times, good times.

Anyway, no more of that for me now. In fact, I'm trying to figure out what got into me when I acted like that. The talking cure seems to be helping me get a handle on it, but I'm worried: last week my therapist suggested we sit in silence for an hour. When I protested, he said, "OK, no talking." And he had a roll of duct tape on his desk . . .

The Monologues
March 11, 2009

     We send our children to college, but we're the ones who get educated.

     Last weekend we traveled up to Minnesota to see our younger daughter in a show that celebrates a part of a woman's body which normally doesn't figure in casual conversation, or in any conversation, really, outside of her ob/gyn's office. These are "The V. Monologues."

     Our daughter attends a small Swedish Lutheran school in the midst of Minnesota Nice farm country, so you younger parents might be surprised to learn that "The V. Monologues" had infiltrated this far. Oh, my sweet innocents: do not be surprised if the Monologues become incorporated into the Robert Crown Health curriculum for the public schools within a decade.

     The drive to Minnesota is always enlightening. Despite the harsh weather, there are no potholes on any, any Minnesota roads. How can this be? Maybe we Illinoisans need more Scandinavian Lutheran road builders. Ja, sure.

     Because my husband and I are hapless nerds, we pass the time in the car listening to Teaching Company lectures on Beethoven's symphonies. For a break, of course, you can listen to any of the 5000 NPR stations in Wisconsin and Minnesota: the minutes will fly like hours.

     By the way, a new outcropping in the Upper Midwest landscape over the last few years is the emergence of those monster windmill farms, reminiscent of Saddam's crossed scimitars or that giant Christ at the Crossroads cross downstate: monuments meant to stupefy the onlooker. No thanks: real farms and real people should have real windmills, not those blowhard behemoths. (Needless to say, our older daughter -- the greenhouse gas gal, the one who can recite large portions of the Kyoto Protocol from memory -- has a different view.)

     Finally, we arrive on campus, and head to the auditorium. A

few other parents were in attendance as well, so once again I marveled at the sight of tall, gentle, stooped, balding men in beautiful Scandinavian sweaters (men no doubt descended from savage Norsemen swinging bloody battle-axes over their heads) on campus for the weekend, allowing their college children to lead them into Indian restaurants to try food they would never choose for themselves.

These dads-in-sweaters pick at the tikki marsala and pick up the tab for it, because they love their kids, kids who have piercings in their eyebrows and beautiful straight teeth because the dads-in-sweaters made sure they wore braces in high school, and the dads picked up the tab for those too, because they love their kids.

In return, the girls gleefully participate in a performance in which they employ words, gestures and topics which cause their dads to blush and stare at the floor for most of the evening. Great job, girls. I hope your kids make you just as proud.

What can you do? We got our daughter flowers and a card on which we had written, "We support the arts!", but because we were writing it in the car, the handwriting was a little shaky, and she thought it said,"We support the ants!"

She hugged us, thanked us for coming, then said, "I love you, but I don't get it."

Our sentiments exactly.

True Lies
June 17, 2009

If you are in the habit of reading this column to the kids, stop now. Tell them this week's article is about mortgage rates, or the state's unfunded pension liabilities, or some other boring subject, or, heck, make up something else. That will get you in shape for this week's real topic: lying to your children.

It starts out innocently enough, of course. When they're babies, you soothe their fussiness with lies like, "Shh, shh, go to sleep, everything's all right," when you really mean, "Shh, shh, I'm so sleep-deprived I can't see straight, I haven't showered in days, it will be a miracle if you escape from infancy alive."

As with any athletic exercise, you become more proficient at lying the more you do it. I encourage you to experiment a little. Lie outside the box. Harken back to your childhood: your parents surely pulled some doozies on you that you could recycle with your kids. Think of it as the Circle of Lie.

Take air conditioning. When I was a kid, we didn't have air conditioning. No one had air conditioning. It was an unimaginable luxury enjoyed only by people like the Monopoly monocle guy. It wasn't until I was in high school that my folks got a window unit, for their bedroom, of course, a room the kids were not ordinarily allowed into.

Our parents supplied us with many reasons for not getting central A.C., none of which involved the truth, namely, that it was too expensive. The chief reason we were given was that it's important to sweat, because sweating is the body's way of ridding itself of dangerous toxins. A.C. prevents you from sweating, thus allowing those poisons to build up until they get to the Red Alert level on the toxin dial, at which point you apparently start oozing slime out of every sweat gland and orifice you possess.

It wasn't quite clear why the toxic sweat analysis didn't apply to our own parents in their chilled bedroom, but we somehow connected it to their use of 5-Day Deodorant Pads (a product I believe is no longer on the market, and rightly so).

Thus, we didn't have A.C. because it was hazardous to your health. Interestingly, it turns out that my husband's parents also used the toxic sweat approach in their anti-air-conditioning campaign. It was consistent with their approach to sickness in general, which often involved "sweating it out."

Perhaps you'd like to update the dialogue, while impressing the kids with how with-it you are, by explaining that you're minimizing the A.C. in order to shrink the family's carbon footprint. Be my guest. It might even be true. In any event, it sounds cooler than, "We're trying to spend less and save more, because the economy is tanking." But beware: next week we may be told by our president that we need to spend more, not less, because the economy is tanking. You need to choose your lies carefully, to avoid being caught between Barack and a hard place.

Similarly, you may decide you need to cut back on ordering out. Now, when I was a kid, nobody I knew ever, ever ordered food to be picked up or delivered. It would have violated the natural order of things: if a restaurant makes it, you eat it at the restaurant; if you make it, you eat it at home, or at a potluck. The idea of bringing the restaurant's food home was as goofy as bringing our food to a restaurant.

The universal parental reason for never ordering take-out or fast food was, "You don't know what they're putting in that stuff." Just pause for a moment to contemplate the underlying premise: "Only food scrutinized and prepared by your ever-vigilant mother in the hyper-sanitary sanctity of our own kitchen will be fit for your consumption." Wow: talk about a whopper.

Anywho, as your kids hurtle toward adulthood, the tenor of your lies changes, reverting to the soothing tones of infancy: "Don't worry, we're OK; the tests came back mostly negative; your father doesn't usually drive like that; I put the skillet in the freezer for a reason;" etc.

So, don't be afraid to lie to your kids. Embrace your inner liar. We teach by example. How else will they learn to be adults, much less parents, if you aren't a good role model liar? Trust me on this, young parents.

Would I lie to you?

Thanksgiving Again?
November 25, 2009

It turns out that a lot of you really like the traditional Thanksgiving foods that I mocked and scorned so mercilessly last week. Who knew there were so many fans of my nemesis, the green bean casserole? OK, I get it. You can quit sending me your secret recipes, because your e-mail, like the casserole itself, is just getting dumped straight into my trash.

Instead of discussing holiday food some more, today we will find out that we have something else in common, namely, the Thanksgiving relatives, the ones you see about as often as the Thanksgiving menu.

As mentioned last week in the promo for this week's column, the relative we'll start with is The Cool Aunt. Sometimes the C.A. is young and heedless of danger, occasionally bringing to the feast a type of stuffing which varies from the kind served at your family's table since Moses brought the recipe down from Mount Sinai. Sausage and cinnamon stuffing from this cool Moroccan cookbook she found while traveling? Oh, honey, no, we're Protestant: the only time sausage and cinnamon can touch each other is at breakfast.

When you're a kid, the Cool Aunt is the only one who gets you genuinely hip articles of clothing and accessories. She's also the only one you can confide in without fear of retribution.

Her own kids, of course, do not appreciate her. I was shocked to learn, at my mother's funeral, that my cousins had thought she was a Cool Aunt. "I could talk to your mom about anything," my cousin Polly sighed. My mom? I couldn't tell her anything. But, of course, she wasn't my aunt.

Another archetypal relative is the uncle who assigns himself the task of herding the children. He's sort of the Kindly Uncle counterpart to the Cool Aunt, but, oddly, the K.U. and the C.A. are rarely married to each other, at least in my family. The Kindly Uncle plays freeze tag with the kids in the backyard while the rest of the adults sit around and drink cocktails and talk about boring stuff.

Then, during dinner itself, he leaves the grown-up table periodically and comes over to the card tables where the kids have been quarantined (so that no adult has to actually watch a child eat, since that is the fastest appetite-killer known to man). "It's a little quiet in there," he explains to his fellow adults as he pushes his chair back. "I'd better go check on the munchkins." The other parents are glad to cede responsibility to him.

He plays Got-Your-Nose with the little ones, and helps them use their knife and fork. He helps everyone finish their vegetables by teaching them how to eat their peas with honey on a knife. "Just don't tell your mom," he warns smilingly.

Of course, no meal would be complete without the Opinionated Relative. He's the one who insists on loudly broadcasting his (unsolicited) views, usually on politics, generally finding the most offensive way to do so. It never occurs to him that anyone would disagree with him, because in fact he rarely hears a discouraging word. Arguing with him is just pouring gasoline on the flame, so most of the time the rest of the table sits in passive resistance to his obnoxiousness.

By the way, the Opinionated Relative can hail from anywhere on the political spectrum. In my husband's family was a right-wing extremist who based his views on what he read in the National Enquirer; in contrast, the family business' bookkeeper, who was always invited to family gatherings for obvious reasons, was a devout Communist who brought issues of Soviet Life for everybody to peruse. Dinners were dynamic, I guess.

What other relatives are there? Actually, the larger the gathering, the more likely it is that you'll have an Unknown Relative, one who has shown up for so many years that now you can't ask who he is. He probably isn't a relative at all. The only people who can question his familial credentials are the very young ("Who dat?") or the very old ("I've never seen that man before in my life. Who on earth is he?" "Grandma, hush.").

And then there are the usual assortment of shirttail relatives, crazy uncles, tipsy aunts, bratty nephews, etc. Happy Thanksgiving to all! Onward to Christmas!

You Say Obama, I Say Omaha
May 5, 2010

As my 88-year-old aunt said after our recent family reunion, "It was a lovely party. Now you don't have to come to the funeral." Don't you hope you're that jaunty at 88? How about 58?

It had been 18 years since this crowd had gotten together, at the wedding of the youngest cousin. Someone had thoughtfully brought the 1982 group wedding pictures to this 2010 reunion, providing the cousins' children with many opportunities to point and howl at hair and clothing styles. Just wait, my pretties. Your kids will be mocking your fashion sense before you know it. After all, everybody loves raiment.

The reunion took place in Omaha, and before you start making ignorant remarks, let me tell you what a beautiful city it is, with a supercool downtown shopping area, gorgeous old residential neighborhoods and congenial natives, many of whom I am not related to. Plus, the airport is well run, and staffed by friendly Nebraskans and Iowans, who are almost as self-effacing and nice as Minnesotans, but slightly less Lutheran.

The reunion was convened to celebrate the above-mentioned aunt's 65th wedding anniversary (and her husband's, my uncle's, as well, but I guess that's understood). 65! Can you imagine? I'm not sure Nebraska was a state when they tied the knot.

The first phase of the reunion was at a downtown pub, so we all quickly lubricated ourselves to get over the 18-year shyness. That didn't take long. The following afternoon the herd reconvened at one of the Omaha cousins' house (the one who played for the 'Huskers at an Orange Bowl lo, these many years ago). As we milled around in the backyard, the unmistakable sound (and it's a BIG sound) of bagpipes hit our ears.

Did I mention that my oldest cousin, a mild-mannered Wisconsin pediatrician, had, several years earlier, become intrigued with the family's Scottish heritage, and had taken to wearing full Scots regalia, kilt and all, at important occasions, including his kids' weddings and, yes, family reunions?

He had also learned to play the bagpipes really well, and his piping march into the backyard was captured for posterity on numerous camera-phones. Kids, don't try this at home.

At the dinner that night, in the banquet room of the Dundee Presbyterian Church (we do take our heritage seriously), some of the boisterous alpha male wannabes trumpeted that there would be a Liberal Table to which the more suspect members of the clan would be consigned.

The Wisconsin pediatrician and his wife, whose support of Barack made them instant black sheep, sat down there at once, retorting that you can't spell Omaha without Obama. Wait...

My brother, who, judging from the tone and content of the e-mail messages he Forwards to me, is a Tea Party activist, immediately boomed that his sister, i.e., me, and her family all belonged there as well. (As my children noted at the time, only in this crowd could Mom be classified as a liberal). Another cousin, a university professor whom I suspect of being a black sheep, tried to fight her way to the Liberal Table, but didn't move fast enough.

Surprisingly, my Tea Party brother and his perfectly nice wife seated themselves with us, to the dismay of the other alphas, who taunted him. He growled, "It's a free country. Nobody tells me where to sit." Philosophical consistency, you see.

All too soon, the weekend was over, and amidst much exchanging of e-mail addresses, the crowd dispersed back from whence they had come. On the flight home, my husband characterized my family as something akin to a Norman Rockwell painting (he meant it as a compliment), contrasting it with his own extended family, whose get-togethers tended to involve much shouting and tablepounding. No matter: the important thing is that family takes you out of yourself and makes you part of something larger.

See, there's no "I" in family. Wait...

P.S. A special shout-out to my dentist, Jerry Scharfenberg, for coming to my rescue! 36 hours before our flight was set to leave for Omaha, the cap on one of my top front teeth cracked and fell out, rendering me a dead ringer for Mayella Ewell of *To Kill a Mocking-*

bird. Dr. Jerry managed to fabricate a temporary cap -- in an acceptable color, even! -- and install it in time for takeoff. Blessings on him, his staff and the patients who got rescheduled on short notice so he could work on me! Thanks to all!

Clean Up Woman
July 21, 2010

  If you can't tell the difference between clean and dirty dishes, you probably shouldn't be the guy in charge of unloading the dishwasher. To divvy up the household chores any other way is simply beating your head against the wall.

  (Actually, head-beating is one of my favorite exercises. Just the other night, I was slamming my noggin against the old drywall when I noticed that the wall was dusty. How can dust collect on a vertical surface? Can't I even rely on the law of gravity to do its fair share? Pull its own weight, as it were? Must I do everything around here?)

  My late mother was a world-class head beater, because she had this unreasonable expectation that her kids should be able to perceive when things needed to be cleaned, put away, vacuumed, etc., Without Being Told. It was doubly unreasonable because she had the highest standards of cleanliness, neatness, etc., of anyone since the dawn of time, when the memory of man runneth not to the contrary.

  My brother and I were always happy to help (and by "happy," I mean "reluctant"), but we needed to be told what to do. In detail. Each time. Otherwise, we assumed that everything was A-OK, and that we could watch TV while Mom vacuumed. Hey, we lifted our feet to allow her to vacuum under the couch. That constitutes helping, doesn't it?

  One of Mom's favorite ploys was to leave clean laundry stacked neatly on the stairs going up to the second floor. The message that she intended to send by doing so: "Hey, I've toiled for hours in the basement, washing, bleaching, drying, starching, ironing and folding your stuff. [She was known to iron my dad's boxers; not sure whether she starched them; not sure whether he even wanted them ironed.] I brought it all up to the first floor, but maybe you guys could finish the job by delivering it to the right place, Without Being Told."

The message my brother and I received: Mom must have forgotten to take the laundry up. Or maybe she had some good reason for leaving it here on the steps. Whatever. So we'd carefully step around the piles as we went up and down and up and down. Finally we'd notice that Mom was giving us the silent treatment, but we wouldn't know why, until eventually her intended message came out, through pursed lips and gritted teeth. Oops.

Her never-ending quest to have her kids learn how to read her mind guaranteed that she would spend a good chunk of her life beating her head against a wall. Poor Mom. She kept a beautiful home, but it came at a great psychic price to all of us, especially her.

I vowed that when I had kids, I'd do things differently. (If we had a nickel for every one of those vows, eh?) Then one day I found myself vacuuming under the couch my kids were sitting on as they stared, transfixed, at the TV and lifted their little feet to accommodate me, craning their necks around so as not to miss a moment of a show they had already seen, oh, probably three hundred times. Were they expecting that this time, Jem and the Holograms would <u>not</u> vanquish Pizzazz and the Misfits?

I turned the TV off. "I could use some help here," I growled through pursed lips and gritted teeth. "After all, it's your sleepover I'm cleaning up for."

They looked around, puzzled. "Everything looks fine, Mom," they chirped, and reached for the remote. I stood amazed. Were they perhaps inhabiting a parallel universe, or OppositeLand, where "Everything looks fine" means "Dust bunnies, dead ahead! Capt'n! There's too many of 'em! The engine's overheatin'! She's gonna blow!"

I grabbed the remote. "Humor me," I hissed. Being of a different generation than mine, however, they were not as cowed by parental authority as I had been. "You don't need to get upset, Mom. Just tell us what you want us to do."

"You should be able to see what needs to be done," I shrieked, "Without Being Told."

Oops. Like the sound of one hand clapping, the sound you make as you slowly morph into your mother is quiet, but unmistakable. I handed the remote back to the kids. "Never mind," I whispered. "A few dust bunnies won't ruin a sleepover, will they?"

The kids didn't answer, having already transferred their attention back to Jem and Pizzazz. That night at the sleepover, one of the guests had to take extra medicine because of her dust allergies.

I never liked her anyway.

Section 7: Food, Glorious Food

Food For Thought, Or America, What's Cookin'?
August 22, 2007

I read recently that, for a healthy diet, you shouldn't eat anything your grandmother wouldn't recognize. The idea behind this is to eliminate modern, highly processed foods (Hot Pockets, Tater Tots: you know, the stuff that tastes good) and concentrate on nourishing food from the garden (broccoli, spinach, blah blah blah: you know, the stuff that tastes good for you).

The author of that piece of advice must have had a different grandma than I did. Mine fed me fish sticks and taught me how to play poker, so that decades later, when I would see *Casino Royale* (sigh), I would actually understand what was going on during the card game. Well, except for the "big blind" thing: I still don't get that.

In any event, the point today is to analyze America's changing tastes in food, and to do this, we must recall what America was really eating in the Good Old Days. I own a 1943 <u>Joy of Cooking</u> cookbook, so I can tell you.

We weren't eating enchiladas, amigo . . . although the recipe for pureed avocado sounds a lot like guacamole. Instead, America was celebrating its soon-to-be-post-war status as a world power by digging into:

<u>Fricassee of Rabbit</u>: I should have stopped reading this recipe after the first line, which is, "Clean and cut into pieces: A rabbit," because the rest of the recipe reminded me of that scene from *Fatal Attraction*; no, not <u>that</u> scene; anyway, the ingredient list does call for two sprigs of parsley, as a cheery garnish, no doubt.

<u>Calf Brains in Blankets</u>: Like pigs in blankets, only . . . different; the kids loved 'em, I'm sure.

<u>Collops of Veal</u>: I don't think it's a good sign when you have

to look up dinner in a dictionary ... AND IT'S NOT THERE. I finally had to resort to the Oxford English Dictionary to learn that "collop" is a British word for a slice of meat. And we wonder why they lost the empire.

<u>Snipe</u>: Broiled, roasted or smothered? Have it your way, just like at Burger King. What's that you say? Another trip to the dictionary? Silly goose: snipe is in the same category as squab, of course. Again, the initial line of directions in the recipe is revealing: "Pick, draw and clean (the French do not draw)." Do we detect an attitude about our wartime ally here, a certain je ne sais quoi? And, by the way, the "draw" here is not, like, sketch-draw; it's like drawn-and- quartered.

<u>Green Peas:</u> I became confused when the recipe did not start with, "Open the freezer," and instead said, "Wash, then hull: one pound of peas." The only hull I know about played for the Black Hawks.

<u>Eggplant Filled With Left Over Food</u>: That is the name of the recipe, folks. Sounds as if the cook, in a pinch, might have swept the floor and emptied the dustpan directly into the eggplant shells. Who'd know?

<u>Tomato Pancakes</u>: You say potato, I say tomato. "Serve them with or without syrup," urges the recipe, strongly implying that it really, really wouldn't matter. The cookbook notes bravely that these "have an attractive red brown color." Going down <u>and</u> coming up, I'll bet.

These recipes do a lot to explain why there was no obesity problem back then. One sees little danger of overeating, does one? Must have been rather easy, in fact, to push oneself away from that table. Gives the phrase "groaning board" a whole new meaning.

This stuff was not, remember, from the Eternally Tacky Fifties, but from the Greatest Generation Forties, OK? Maybe there was a reason so many guys volunteered to go off to war: got 'em away from Ma's cookin'. By the way, I spared you the Wartime Emergency Soups, all of which sound like they were concocted by starving Russians in the last phase of the Siege of Stalingrad.

Well, bon appetit, I guess. I gotta go: it's almost suppertime, and those calf brains won't cook themselves!

What Happens In The Fridge, Stays In The Fridge
November 14, 2007

So ... has enough time passed for us to have a sense of humor about the August storm / power outage / tree damage catastrophe?

I didn't think so.

One thing about a prolonged power outage: it really brings to the surface everyone's opinions about the refrigeration of food. Now, that's not a topic you even think you have an opinion about ...until the fridge conks out.

Only then do you discover the omissions of that pre-Canna conferencing you went through before marriage. Frequency of sex? Having kids? Believing in God? Those are minor issues you can work out on the job.

But the significance of the date stamped on perishable food? That's a deal-breaker.

The whole topic starts out innocently enough, early on, when you're dating and thus trying to suppress your natural obnoxiousness. You go to your future mother-in-law's house for dinner and notice that a butter dish holding a stick of room temperature butter is always on the table.

If you were brought up on the notion that a refrigerator is a life-support device into which all food must be crammed (including, for example, uncooked spaghetti still in the box), that darn butter dish is troublesome.

The voice in your head - you know the one I'm talking about - is screaming, "Butter! That's a dairy product, man! Like eggs and mayonnaise and mustard and corned beef! The stuff you pack in ice on a picnic because it will KILL you if it comes even close to room temperature!"

Then the other voice in your head - there are so many sometimes - says calmly, "That is his mom. Don't insult her or him or her housekeeping practices. Obviously the family members survived years of room temperature butter. ("Well, the STRONG ones survived," sneers your first voice.) Don't make a fuss."

So you swallow hard, and smile, and eventually get married and have kids. Soon you start noticing things. Little things. You're straightening up the contents of the refrigerator, evicting the squatters who've clearly overstayed their welcome, and you run across some unopened yogurt cups stamped with a date in the not-too-distant past.

You regretfully put them on the counter, to begin their journey out of your life, and then find shortly thereafter that they've mysteriously returned to the fridge. Your spouse shrugs: "That yogurt's still good. Those dates are just guidelines, really."

The screaming voice in your head pipes up on cue: "Guidelines? GUIDELINES? Is E. coli a guideline? Why do you think they call it a DIE date?"

These minor skirmishes continue until one day - say, in August 2007 - you have the super duper power outage, and you have to employ a triage method of sorting through the stuff in the refrigerator after the power eventually returns. You make your opening move: "Well, clearly, all the dairy stuff has to get pitched."

Your spouse sniffs inside the carton of milk, which has been sitting opened in a dead refrigerator for 36 hours, and shrugs: "Smells OK to me. You know, a fridge is heavily insulated. Stuff stays pretty cold in there for a long time."

How did you overlook this drastic character flaw before you got married? The butter on his mother's table should have been a big red warning flag - with a skull and crossbones on it.

You tell your screaming voice to shut up, you smile sweetly, and later (OK, in the dead of night) you sneak downstairs and quietly pour the rest of the milk down the sink. Your spouse is awake when you return, and you coyly whisper, "I just had a midnight snack of cookies and milk. You were right about the milk. It was so good I finished it all off."

He clutches you anxiously: "Really? Because I was just thinking you were probably right about the milk. Hope you'll be OK."

The secret to a happy marriage? A 5000-watt generator in the garage, so you can keep the fridge going at all costs.

Sally Sotos and her husband also have differing opinions about expired medicines.

Countdown to Christmas
September 17, 2008

Now that Labor Day is well behind us, and Columbus Day is just around the bend, we all know what we need to do. Plant the spring bulbs in the garden? Begin the fall housecleaning?

Please.

No: it is time to recognize that we must buckle down and join the pre-holidays diet frenzy, sprinting toward our fighting weight these last weeks before Halloween. If you're not down to the lowest weight you can sustain (while still summoning the energy to bring fork to mouth) by trick-or-treat night, you're sunk. After that, it's a madcap whirl of overeating for the next two months ... or three months, if you deem the Superbowl the official end of the Christmas season. (Different denominations have different takes on this issue.)

Actually, Halloween itself is the kick-off of the pigging-out. Somehow this holiday has evolved from a straightforward night of devil worship into a weekend of Superbowl-type parties in which we compete to see how many orange-and-black-frosted goodies we can ingest without blowing out the elastic in our undergarments. Halloween itself is on a Friday night this year, so expect to find yourself waking up on Monday morning feeling like Ray Milland in *Lost Weekend*.

From there, it's less than four weeks 'til Thanksgiving, which is on a Thursday this year. But don't expect to make up any lost ground during those four weeks. Instead, your time will be spent finishing the leftovers from the satanic bacchanalia you attended and/or hosted, occasionally propping yourself up on one elbow to put your Mr. and Mrs. Turkey Pilgrim salt and pepper shakers on the table, as a gesture toward decorating for the holiday. And this year, would you please try to remove the Halloween lights before Christmas? The neighbors are having enough trouble selling their house, as it is.

(A brief moment of silence at this point in the calendar, as we pause to recall that the next James Bond movie is due to be released

-- or shall we say unleashed? -- between Halloween and Thanksgiving. Some of us may try to shed a few pounds before that day, on the off chance that Willis Johnson of Classic Cinemas has secretly arranged for Daniel Craig to attend the premiere at the York Theater in Elmhurst. You never know . . .)

Then we arrive at Thanksgiving Day, and demonstrate our manifest destiny to consume more calories per capita than any other nation on Earth. We'll spend the first several days after Thanksgiving detoxing, weaning ourselves off turkey by transitioning from turkey sandwiches to turkey casserole to turkey soup, finally joining the dog in the backyard to fight over who gets to gnaw on the drumstick.

Only 28 days -- four little weekends -- separate Thanksgiving from Christmas this year, meaning that for sure there will be times when you have to go to holiday parties more than once per weekend! Some of us aren't used to such an action-packed schedule, but the prospect of eating on someone else's dime definitely helps ease the pain. You throw yourself into the death-spiral of over-consumption, promising yourself that, once the new year comes, things will be different, and you won't have to wear that muu-muu so much.

We know all of this is going to happen, so let's plan ahead. My friends, let's start now. Not eating; I mean, start dieting! There's still time to shrink that stomach! Ask not for whom the dinner-bell tolls; it tolls for me . . .

Come and Get It!
November 12, 2008

Does your dinner table look like Madison Avenue's version? You know: smiling, handsome Daddy and Mommy serving food to two cute and happy kids (one of each gender -- don't want to offend anyone). They appear to be looking forward to having dinner together at the same time, all eating the same thing.

Are they pod people? Do they walk among us, disguised as humans?

For comparison, let's look at a real family dinner table. Right off the bat, one kid is missing because she's at (pick two): play practice/choir rehearsal / basketball tryouts / detention hall / the boyfriend's house, trying to disable the GPS tracker on her car.

The family remnant who actually show up (reluctantly) for dinner bear only a faint resemblance to the image portrayed in American advertising, a fact I realized as I assessed my own table recently...starting with myself.

Instead of a smiling TV Mommy, lovingly passing around heaping helpings of mashed potatoes, our family's mommy sits glumly contemplating her bowl of low-cal canned soup and plate of limp tossed salad, topped with exactly ten pre-measured spray doses of Wishbone Salad Disinfectant...I mean, Salad Spritzer, scowling while she fills out her Weight Watchers meal plan chart.

Mommy turns grimly to Daddy and bitterly surveys his fare, which consists of a bowl of labna (sort of a Middle Eastern mutant offspring of yogurt and sour cream) into which he has dumped peanuts, raisins and pickled beets, alongside a plate of olives and feta cheese. Opaa. Mommy reflects that, decades ago, this same meal had struck her as exotic and reminiscent of Omar Sharif and Zorba the Greek. Now, it just brings on her usual wave of nausea. How can he keep that stuff down? The man must have a cast-iron stomach.

Daddy looks over at Older Daughter's plate, and sighs. O.D.'s meal, what we call the Marrakesh Express, contains lentils, whole grain pasta and broccoli. It tastes as good as it sounds. She washes it down with copious drafts of soy milk. She is lactose-intolerant; we are lentil-intolerant.

O.D. does not wish to partake of much of anything we have around the house, as it does not promote the sustainable lifestyle she endorses. So she essentially keeps kosher in her parents' home, with separate foods and reusable glass containers for her leftovers (apparently my Tupperware has something ghastly and toxic in the plastic which will eventually kill us all, except for O.D., who one day will find her parents slumped on the kitchen floor, plastic food containers on the counter, and O.D. will carefully step over our bodies on her way out the door, turn, say, "Told you so," and head off to her job as chief of President Obama's Environmental Protection Agency. Kids do the darndest things.)

Our missing family member, Younger Daughter, with access to what has become the best food in the world -- college dorm food -- prefers to feast on pickles and cream cheese, wrapped in cotto salami. We used to imagine that our kids would get an apartment together someday, but the prospects for that are looking grim, wouldn't you say? Kind of like jamming matter and anti-matter into the same jar, our kids preparing their dinners in the same kitchen at the same time would cause a rift in the space-time continuum.

In any event, it is clear that the truth-in-advertising laws do not extend to Madison Avenue's portrayal of the American dinner hour, which is just as well: the real thing would probably cause us to lose our appetites, thus defeating the purpose of the advertising.

Or am I wrong?

For those of you still reeling from the results of the presidential election, just think about it this way: after saddling our children (and their children) with gazillions of dollars of debt, the least we can do is let them have the president they want. He seems like a nice fella. Could stand to bulk up a bit, though. Maybe we'll invite him to dinner . . .

A Christmas Lesson
December 17, 2008

There's something about Christmas shopping during a recession that can bring out the Scrooge in all of us. Or maybe the Grinch. People you resent shopping for in the best of times are really going to suffer this year, aren't they?

Like they care. They don't even send you a thank-you note, or a thank-you e-mail. You're lucky if you get a thank-you text message ("Tnx 4 t bk." You're welcome, honey.) Well, they're going to pay for that behavior in a few days, by gosh. This shopping list just got a wee bit shorter.

Hey, now I'm really in the Christmas spirit! The Ebenezer Scrooge spirit, that is, pre-Marley's visit.

I mentioned this attitude problem of mine to my husband recently, and he took it all in stride. "You don't know the meaning of suffering through a holiday," he boomed. "You can't know: you're a Protestant! From Glen Ellyn! You think holidays were made for enjoyment and family togetherness and wearing long stocking caps while you ice skate at night on Lake Ellyn! You grew up in a snow-globe!"

I shrank in fear from his Greek Orthodox wrath. His theory, as it turned out, was that holidays were not made for enjoyment. They were meant instead for suffering, to remind us of what a good deal we had during the rest of the year, by demonstrating how bad things could easily be.

For example: "You probably had extra food around the house before Christmas, didn't you, missy?" he thundered. "Little ginger snaps and sugar cookies shaped like elf shoes? Well, we had <u>less</u> food around, because we had to fast. And not just any fast: a graduated fast, to make the suffering last longer.

A graduated fast is like this. Say Christmas is on a Sunday. Starting on Thursday, you stop eating meat. On Friday, you stop eating dairy products. By Saturday night you're on bread and water, same as if you were in a Turkish prison."

And his family didn't break the fast until they got home from the lengthy midnight church service and had a full meal -- at 2 a.m. And not just any meal: this was a special fish dish, plaki, something to do with halibut in a raisin sauce. And they met the fish challenge head-on, shall we say, so that the raisins and the fish-eyes were indistinguishable from each other, floating together in the sauce. "Didn't have that in Glen Ellyn, did you?" he sneered.

"Stop! Stop, oh spirit of Christmas past!" I sobbed, clutching my stomach and retching. "We had strata at 10 a.m. made from day-old white bread soaked overnight in eggs and then baked to a golden brown!"

My husband snorted derisively. "And what did that teach you? Nothing! It made you resentful that you didn't have strata more often! But plaki taught us to be grateful that we didn't have plaki more often! Resentment or gratitude: which is the better holiday lesson?"

I hung my head in shame, and restored my nephew's name to my shopping list. Maybe he wasn't such a bad kid after all, despite his text messages.

And that is how I learned the true meaning of the season: be grateful. Christmas comes but once a year.

Just Desserts
December 31, 2008

At a loss for what to whip up as a festive holiday dish? Me neither. Nevertheless, it's always worthwhile perusing my 1943 edition of Irma Rombauer's Joy of Cooking, particularly if you need a break from staring out the window at our interminable winter weather ("Stay at home, for God's sake! Incredibly dangerous driving conditions! Details at ten!"). But back to the cookbook...

The chapter on "Luncheon and Supper Dishes" lured me in when the introduction to the recipe for creamed veal admonished, "There is no reason why this dish should not be delicious." Creamed veal? No reason?

This chapter also contains a recipe for "Brunswick Stew," to make your family feel like they're eating at the bowling alley. Again. There are also directions for "Bananas in Blankets," but the blankets turn out to be strips of bacon: Filling All Your Nitrite Needs Since 1943!

Hurrying into the section on Meat, I was captivated by the directions for Roast Suckling Pig, containing appetite-whetting references such as, "Sew up the pig. Put a block of wood in the pig's mouth to hold it open. Cover the ears with pieces of well-greased paper. Secure them with paper clips." Probably the kids loved to help Mom with this one. "No fair! It's my turn to put the paper clips on!"

I stopped reading the recipe for "Sautéed Liver" at the part, "Remove the skin and veins from a calf liver." What am I, chopped liver surgeon? For the same reason, I also skipped the discussion of "Liver Loaf," "Liver Dumplings," and "Liver Breakfast Spread" (the best to you each morning!). The gruesome details of the recipe for "Calf Head Cheese" cannot all be printed in a family newspaper, but they start with, "Remove ears, brains, eyes, snout and most of the fat from a calf head." Our grandmothers were clearly made of sterner stuff than we are.

Feeling queasy, I went straight to the desserts, but wouldn't you know, the first one I ran into was "Steamed Suet Pudding." Imagine marching proudly into the dining room with steaming bowls of stuff you usually hang in the back yard for the birds to eat. You'll pretty much have the table to yourself, I think. It's good around the holidays, though: "Oh, bring us a suet pudding..."

Then there's "Steamed Brown Pudding." What flavor is that? Brown. The taste makers at Jello missed a golden -- or is that golden-brown? -- opportunity to create an instant pudding out of this one. There's always room for Steamed Brown Pudding.

Other tempting offerings from The Joy of Cooking:

Mystery Cake: The secret ingredient is tomato soup. And why not.

Prune Whip: Alert the folks at Cool Whip. This product could combine our need for regularity with our love of overeating: win-win!

Hard Boiled Egg Cookies: The secret ingredient is hard boiled eggs.

Rocks: One can only guess how these cookies earned their name. The recipe is followed immediately by one for Bran Cookies. Perhaps for a reason.

Sand Tarts: The secret ingredient is . . . no, just kidding. Possible marketing strategies: "It's like there's a beach party in my mouth, and everyone's invited!" Or, "Favorite snack of the sand people of Tatooine!"

Emergency Icing: This cookbook has a lot of "Emergency" recipes. Turns out it means "Last Minute" recipes, but at first I thought "Emergency" meant the stuff you cooked when the ambulance pulled up in front of the house. Those EMTs have to eat sometime.

Hopefully the emergency isn't food-related, but if it is, my money's on the suet pudding.

I know I will live to regret this, but I promised my family, so here goes: if you think you might be interested in a reasonably-priced book consisting of a collection of these columns of mine, maybe for Christmas next year, please raise your hand. Good. Now, lower your hand onto your computer keyboard and e-mail me at elmhurstss@aol.com. You're not committing yourself to anything; I'm just looking for a show of hands, so I can decide whether to pursue this. Your e-mail address will not be added to any list, as I don't know how. I will probably end up accidentally deleting it anyway. Thanks!

Battling the Great Depression
January 14, 2009

No, not the economic one. There's nothing we can do about that one, pal. In fact, whatever we do on that front will only make things worse. Didn't you read that the recovery is being delayed because American households are saving their money instead of spending it?

It's Goldilocks time! First, the experts tell us that our excessive purchasing got us into this mess ("Too much spending!"), and now they tell us that our excessive saving is keeping us in the mess ("Not enough spending!"). Unfortunately, unlike Goldilocks, we apparently have no "just right!" option. Whatever we do or say is wrong. Kind of like in a spousal argument.

So, no, battling the Great Depression doesn't involve economic matters. We're talking about the post-holidays depression. For one thing, it's January, so by definition the weather is a downer. For another thing, the ink (or blood, depending on how serious you were) wasn't even dry on your New Year's resolutions before you began breaking them, starting with the one that's always at the top of the list every year, year after year.

You know the one. It pertains to food, and consuming less of it.

There are several approaches to take. For years we had a device attached to our refrigerator door in which this recording was activated whenever the door opened:

"Are you eating again? Shame on you! No wonder you look the way you do! Ha, ha! You'll be sorry, fatty! Do yourself a favor: SHUT THE DOOR!" The recording ended with a maniacal laugh.

Actually, that worked pretty well at first. We'd do anything to avoid hearing that grating voice. But after awhile, it became just another of those "You'll shoot your eye out!" warnings that we all ignore in life. Then we figured out that if you turned your attention to non-refrigerated snacks, you could gorge yourself blissfully and never hear The Voice.

Finally, the batteries in the darn thing wore out, so The Voice got slower and lower, and the message took about three minutes instead of 30 seconds, and wouldn't you know, we just never got around to replacing those batteries. (Same deal with the smoke detector: new batteries would just mean hearing those annoying warnings again. Who needs it?)

But there are other approaches to take to obey your eat-less resolution. One is to stock the larder with food you don't like, so that there's nothing to tempt you. We're doing that now, involuntarily, as our daughter's eggplant, lentils and black beans slowly crowd out our Italian sausage and chocolate syrup. Our refrigerator is an antioxidant waiting to happen.

Even those few vegetables that I like are having to rub shoulders with the nerd vegetables: you know, the ones that would be the last ones chosen to be on your vegetable team. Like lima beans. Wouldn't it be more merciful to simply freeze the nerd foods cryogenically, until medical science finds a cure for them?

Perhaps you don't like this approach either, eh? Not to worry. I just read that there's a new batch of diet books on the market, and one is bound to be perfect for you. I'm captivated by "The Lunch Box Diet:" it advises you to pack a (leakproof -- or is that leekproof?) lunch box of vegetables, meat and secret sauce; take it to work; then, at lunchtime, shake the box vigorously while you jump up and down for five seconds.

Now, where I work, no one would bat an eye, but maybe your place is one of those snooty, stuffed-shirt outfits where some brown-noser would rat you out to HR and put you on psych watch. If so, don't endanger your job security; confine your Lunch Box Diet to the comfort of your own home, where your family members are used to your antics.

They've had you on psych watch for years anyway.

We Brood About Food
April 8, 2009

    Maybe it's the Lenten season, with its spirit of self-denial and fasting and so forth. Or maybe it was watching our younger daughter, home for spring break last week, whipping up her favorite meal of dill pickle slices smothered in cream cheese and wrapped in a piece of cotto salami (Can't imagine why Lunchables hasn't seized on this little taste treat.).

    Whatever the reason, we started obsessing about eating.

    Wait! Now I remember what started it. We were feeding our newly adopted dogs their required serving of duck and rice, on account of their allegedly sensitive stomachs and food allergies. Please: I know a good scam when I see it. "We're sorry, but we can't eat anything except duck and rice. Maybe a little lamb and rice on holidays, but definitely never, never, ever plain old dog food." (And if you try to fool them by slipping in some of that mainstream major brand dog food, they spit it right up, because they caught you sneaking the Alpo in the back door.)

    Anyway, we couldn't help but notice that the dogs were eating duck and rice, whereas we were eating salad and Progresso soup, and we tried to remember the last time we had had duck, or even lamb. It's been awhile. Maybe somebody should tell these dogs there's a recession going on, and it doesn't play very well to be dining on duck while the rest of us are tightening our belts. Then, they have the nerve to beg for seconds! Looking for a bailout, beagle boys? Not until you've digested that first tranche. (Actually, we managed to stretch our dog food dollar by adding some oatmeal to their cuisine, as sort of a Haggis Helper.)

    Well, whatever the reason, we fell to musing about food. Not that we're particularly well qualified to do so, our culinary skills being pretty limited. (Note the reference to canned soup in the above paragraph.) My husband's idea of gourmet dining is a meal of cold steak, feta cheese and beer, consumed while standing over the kitchen sink and watching The Game. Funny, he used to cook elaborate dinners for me all the time when we were dating. The old bake-and-switch, I guess.

So, we've decided that there are two kinds of people in the world: folks who eat leftovers (the majority, I'd guess), and folks who don't (a vocal minority.) We prefer leftovers, figuring they're food that's withstood the test of time, which is true up to a point, until things start to go horribly wrong. The vocal minority regards leftovers as used food, unfit for consumption. By a lucky stroke of fate, our next-door neighbor is an anti-leftover gal who brings over to us whatever her family, including their two dogs, rejects (or maybe she's just downwind of our kitchen exhaust fan, and deduces the obvious, namely, that cooking is not anyone's long suit at Casa Sotos.)

In the meantime, our beagle boys are witnessing all of this with an innocent lack of concern. We speculate that, if told that times are tough for many people, our dogs would paraphrase Marie Antoinette:

Let them eat duck.

My Big Fat Greek Easter
April 29, 2009

"I guess they had good weather for it last night," my husband remarked one recent Sunday morning over coffee. Since there had been no conversation for the preceding twenty minutes, it was difficult to discern who "they" or what "it" was. Indefinite pronoun references, and cryptic remarks generally, are my husband's specialty. It took me years to figure that out, that is, to figure out that I wasn't going crazy, he was; and by that time, I was too. Marriage does that to you. So does being an asylum guard, I suppose.

"What are we talking about, now?" I asked warily, quickly scanning the memory banks to try to decipher the subject matter and determine what "they" had had good weather for: ball game? Tax protest rally? Neighborhood skunk hunt?

My better half shot me a pitying look, the way Charles Boyer would look at Ingrid Bergman when he was trying to drive her crazy in *Gaslight* ("Paula, don't you even remember that brooch?"). "Today's Greek Easter, Sal," explained my husband patiently. "Yes?" "That means last night was the midnight service." "Yes?"

A few more conversational hurdles later, I was finally made to understand that the midnight service ends with the entire congregation, led by the priest, walking through and then outside the church, into the street (Aha! Hence the desire for good weather!) singing "Christus Aneste," while holding lighted candles aloft.

Anyway, we haven't even gotten to the high point yet, which is when everybody goes home and breaks their Lenten fast with a special soup. Alert readers of this column may recall that Greek tradition also has a special fast-break food (no basketball metaphor implied) at Christmas, a fish stew called plaki. At Easter, they throw a change-up (no baseball metaphor implied), a lamb soup called mageiritsa.

This soup is the kind of food Upton Sinclair built his muckraking reputation on when he wrote about the stockyards. It's the reason the Pure Food and Drug Act was adopted by an outraged and slightly nauseated Congress. The recipe itself (this is from a book; I couldn't make this up) says, "Mageiritsa means whatever the cook can come up with from what's left over of the main ingredients of the Easter meal, namely, roast lamb or goat. No part of the animal goes to waste. Some people even use the tripe and feet." Just like the Up-man said: everything but the squeal . . . or the baa.

Hey, strap on your LambCam, we're just getting started. A cousin of Mageiritsa is Kokkoretsi, an appetizer defined in the same recipe book as part of "a typical Easter spread." Let's remember what an appetizer is supposed to do -- whet your appetite, not kill it -- while we read that kokkoretsi means "Skewered, Grilled Mixed Innards."

Space limitations prohibit me from sharing the whole delightful recipe with you, but here's a little tease: "While the liver, spleen, heart, sweetbreads and kidneys from one spring lamb or goat are marinating, wash the intestines and stomach lining thoroughly. To clean the intestines, attach one opening to the faucet and hold with one hand to keep it from popping off. Turn on cold water and let it run gently. Carefully squeeze intestine from top to bottom many times, with water running, so as to clean out all residue thoroughly. Turn inside out, if desired, to clean even more."

I think my favorite part of that is the "if desired." I mean, who wouldn't desire to "clean even more"? A lamb colonoscopy prep was just what I had in mind for the holidays.

And let's not even mention the loads of fun this would be for the kiddies: so much better than a boring old Easter egg hunt, wouldn't you say? "Mom! No fair! Heather's hogging the faucet! It's her turn to marinate the spleen!"

Well, gotta go. Those intestines won't squeeze themselves, you know! But next week we'll definitely start exercising, won't we?

Right after we've polished off the leftover tripe.

If You Like It So Much, YOU Give Thanks!
November 18, 2009

Hollywood director Barry Levinson made a wonderful movie in 1990 called *Avalon*, about the families of three immigrant brothers in Baltimore. One of the recurring themes in the film is that the oldest of the brothers is chronically late, by several hours, for every family gathering, but is mortally insulted when, one Thanksgiving, the rest of the family has tired of waiting for him, and begins the meal in his absence. When he finally arrives, many hours late, he surveys the family members eating at the dining room table and exclaims incredulously, "You cut the turkey without me?"

I think of that line every year around this time, because it captures the two elements which are common to almost everyone's Thanksgiving: oddball food and crazy relatives.

First, the food. Why do we all eat the same thing, year after grinding year? Sure, each family has its own little variations on the main theme -- one family has sage stuffing, another uses walnuts and raisins -- but we're all eating off the same general page . . . or, in this case, the same pre-printed restaurant menu:

"Thursday's Special:

Dry turkey!

Gravy to moisten the dry turkey!

Stuffing, a/k/a wet chunks of bread!

Cranberry relish, because it sounds good in theory!

Your choice of potatoes or yams, to fulfill your body's need for ever-larger portions of starch!

Green beans almondine, or green bean casserole, a truly American way to tart up an otherwise innocuous but healthful vegetable by larding it with equal parts of Campbell's Cream of Mushroom soup glop (fresh from the can!) and French's french-fried onions!

Top off your meal with pumpkin, apple or pecan pie, whichever seems most likely to add the final artery clog!

And don't forget the Cool Whip!"

What's that about? Is that really a line-up you would choose of your own volition? Well, then, why do we do it?

The official myth, I know, is that Thanksgiving is a holiday of remembrance and re-enactment, so that we eat the same meal that our forebears allegedly enjoyed.

Really? I'll bet their turkey wasn't the kind we have, the kind that gets fattened up as if it had spent its life in the Hansel and Gretel witch house. No, the Pilgrims were probably eating wild turkey (not the beverage), which may well have been an improvement on the acorns and elm bark they'd been feasting on previously; but wild turkey sounds as if it's a whole lot gamier-tasting than the stuff we're used to. Venison, anyone?

And our re-enactment of that First Supper is no doubt also slightly inauthentic as to the green bean casserole (archaeologists have yet to unearth evidence of pre-20th century cream of mushroom glop, but if they do, I'm sure it will help explain the hitherto mysterious disappearance of the lost people of the Roanoke colony). Pretty sure they didn't have Cool Whip back then either. Oh, and, BTW, if we're being authentic, let's be authentic: no TV after the big meal. And polish those buckles on your shoes, mister.

Now, the other theory is that the meal is a celebration in which we have a great feast of our choicest foods.

OK, if that's the theory, then why is the centerpiece of the meal (the food centerpiece, I mean, not the ceramic turkey wearing a Pilgrim hat) -- why is the centerpiece of the meal a species which we generally don't regard as primo poultry, and which in fact is used as filler for other, more delicious foods: turkey franks, turkey burgers, turkey bacon? Is turkey really your celebratory food of choice?

"Great game, you guys! Turkey for everyone!"

"Honey, we're so happy that you got a job, your dad and I want to take you out to a nice restaurant for turkey."

"Now that you've won the gold medal, what are you gonna do?" "Whaddya think? I'm gonna eat my way through the frozen turkey section at Jewel!"

No, our celebration food is not a Butterball, it's a Butterburger, or a steak, or a pizza, or anything, really, except turkey. Ditto re yams. And cranberry relish.

So, food is the first thing that's characteristic and confusing about Thanksgiving. The second is the relatives to go along with the crazy food, but I've run out of room. Next time we'll discuss that topic, including my glossary of Everyone's Got One: The Cool Aunt, The Kindly Uncle Who Plays With The Kids Because He Prefers Their Company To That Of Other Adults, etc.

Stay tuned. And don't cut the turkey without me.

Sally Sotos hopes you were able to put up your outdoor Christmas lights on that nice 65-degree weekend we had recently, because it will soon be but a distant memory.

Delectable December Delights
December 2, 2009

We're past Thanksgiving, nodding at Pearl Harbor Day, and hurtling toward Christmas, so it's time to drag out our 1943 edition of Irma Rombauer's <u>Joy of Cooking</u> for some inspiration. This cookbook came out within two years of Pearl Harbor, but let's try to avoid whipping up something that will live in infamy. Best not to make your guests think longingly of the Bataan Death March either.

Well, where shall we start? How about Irma's chapter on vegetables, for some family-pleasing treats? Here, between the recipe for Sweet Potatoes in Orange Cups (it's just what it sounds like, a completely orange-colored dish. Let's re-name it Another Weasley, as they say at Hogwarts) and the recipe for Boiled Cauliflower (it starts, "Soak in cold water, head down, for 30 minutes;" I thought I was reading a hangover remedy). Aha, here's what you were looking for: a recipe for Dasheens.

What are Dasheens, you may ask. Good question. I consulted my trusty Oxford English Dictionary, and . . . no dasheens! Good Lord! Is it a species that has become extinct since 1943, like liberal Republicans? I finally had to turn to the Interweb and Dr. Google to learn that a dasheen is a taro root.

Must I do everything for you? OK: according to the OED (which is a little abashed about leaving out dasheens, and is trying to regain its composure), a taro root is a starchy tropical root-plant, brought back from the Sandwich Islands by Captain Cook in 1769. See? Now you're smarter than you were three paragraphs ago.

We're going to skip over Irma's recipes for Masked Cauliflower (a masked avenger, indeed: grab your Beano) and Beet Cups (a whole pickled beet, hollowed out and filled with horseradish: not even Beano will save you here), and go straight for the Stuffed Brussels Sprouts (filled with French dressing and "any good sandwich spread, such as liver sausage and tomato soup;" doctors use this one to test your gag reflex).

Had enough veggies? Then let's move on to today's seafood

luncheon special: Shrimp Wiggle. People, I'm only the messenger. Actually, don't worry: the shrimp aren't wiggling, although your guests will soon. Irma advises, "Serve the wiggle at once on rounds of hot buttered toast," like that's gonna help, or, she suggests, "The wiggle may be placed in a greased baking dish and covered with cornflakes." Why haven't the good people at Kellogg's picked up on this one? "Brown the top under a broiler." Until it stops wiggling. Then dispose of safely.

Perhaps some ginger ale will settle your stomach; better yet, how about Ginger Ale Salad? On second thought, our dogs eat grass to aid digestion; maybe you should try that.

I'll spare you the Split Pea and Fish Soup recipe, which begins, "This may be made at low cost, as many fish mongers give away fish heads, tails, fins and scraps," and ends, "You will find this soup worth a trial." And a hung jury, self-inflicted.

Come on, folks, we're almost done: I can see light at the end of the broiler. We just need to hack our way through the Salmon Pot Pie (Swanson's? Hello? The time is right!), Emergency Fish Cakes (that should be Emergency Room Fish Cakes) and Steamed Fish Pudding (because the family was getting so tired of that boring chocolate stuff).

Ah, here we are: German Honey Cakes, which sound fine until Irma promises, "These cakes will keep for six months and longer if placed in a closed tin."

And buried in the backyard. Along with your guests.

Hot Town, Summer in the Kitchen
July 14, 2010

The 4th of July has come and gone, so we are now officially in the throes of summer. Numero Uno way to tell it's summer: you had yummy all-American food on the 4th of July. Burgers and hot dogs sizzling on the grill; corn on the cob, dripping with salty butter; baked beans; watermelon with seeds you can spit while the juice runs down your chin. Yay!

Actually, we had Quinoa Bake.

Parents of a certain age know that there's only one reason for that to happen, namely, the vegetarian kid is home for the holidays.

Now, Quinoa Bake isn't all that bad; it's sort of a Third World Hamburger Helper. That is, if you had, or could afford, hamburger, you'd use it instead of quinoa, and this dish would be called a ground beef casserole (or Hamburger Hot Dish, if you're from Minnesota).

But if you couldn't get enough hamburger meat or if, for some inexplicable reason, you deliberately chose not to get hamburger, then, yes, you could choose quinoa. Like any casserole worth its salt, so to speak, QB is really all about the onion, garlic, tomato, cheese, etc., that are its main constituents.

(Quinoa is pronounced KEEN-wa, as in, "We're keen for quinoa," yet another example of a non-English word being given an English spelling which makes no phonetic sense; see, for example, the Chinese word "Qing." Now, who picked that spelling for a word pronounced, roughly, "Ching"? I'm just asking.)

The point is, we began bantering about what the vegetarian's late grandmothers would have thought about Quinoa Bake, which led, as such conversations always do, to our 1943 edition of Irma Rombauer's Joy of Cooking. What would Irma serve on a hot summer day? We soon found out (gulp):

*Orange and Bermuda Onion Salad: Which consists, strangely, of orange sections and thin slices of Bermuda onion, artfully arranged on lettuce leaves and served, nay, probably drenched, with French dressing.

*Kidney or Lima Bean Salad: I'm hoping she means, "Kidney Bean or Lima Bean Salad." The alternative is too dreadful to contemplate; however, it may explain Irma's editorial comment, "Men like the heft of this." All men? Or just Hannibal Lecter?

*Japanese Persimmons: Shouldn't we be skeptical of a recipe which begins, "This is an attractive-looking salad"? Isn't the unspoken follow-up, "Sure, it _looks_ good, but . . . yikes!" Or is Irma striking a courageous blow for post-war peace and harmony simply by including a recipe with the word "Japanese" in it? Maybe she should have called them "Freedom Persimmons."

*Panned Oysters: Usually my cooking is panned _after_ people have had a bite of it, so naming it this way is sort of a preemptive strike . . . Actually, I ran across Panned Oysters after contemplating:

*Buttered Oysters: Please note the unusual tone throughout this short recipe: "This is recommended as an excellent dish, quickly prepared. With grapefruit halves, rusks and a beverage it is an ideal emergency lucheon [misspelling in original]." You heat up the oysters, slap some butter and salt on 'em, and then, "Serve them at once."

What's your hurry, sister? Not even time for proof-reading? (Or maybe there is such a meal as "lucheon.") I feel like Irma whipped this one up one day when her husband came home for lunch unexpectedly, and she had to stash someone in the root cellar until Hubby went back to work.

Note how she doesn't even tell us what rusks are. I had to look them up. And now, so do you. Let's just say they're not what I'd match up with grapefruit halves. (You have to look up quinoa too; this column comes with homework assignments.)

Nor does she specify what "beverage" she has in mind for this "emergency lucheon." A couple of belts in the middle of the day probably helped pass the time in 1943. Still do.

Well, it's summertime, and the livin' is easy. So relax. Treat yourself to some buttered oysters and quinoa, then crack open a cold one. You'll need it.

About the Author:

Sally Sotos is a mother, wife, attorney and columnist for the Elmhurst Independent. She graduated from Glenbard West High School (Glen Ellyn, IL), Miami University (Ohio) and Loyola University School of Law (Chicago), in that order. She has been practicing law since 1977, and writing humor columns since 2005. Sally and her husband, George, a lawyer currently serving time as a judge, reside in Elmhurst, Illinois with their beagles, Wally and Aidan. Sally and George have two daughters: Mary, a St. Olaf College graduate, lives in Washington, D.C. and works for World Resources Institute; Maggie, a Gustavus Adolphus College graduate, lives in Minneapolis and ekes out a living as an improv actor and playwright.

Made in the USA
Charleston, SC
26 December 2010